Your Chinese Horoscope for the Year of the Dragon

February 5th 2000

to

January 23rd 2001

Asia 2000 Ltd
&
Maison d'éditions Quaille
Hong Kong

© 1999 Maison d'éditions Quaille

ISBN 962-7160-08-3

Published by Asia 2000 Ltd
302 Seabird House
22-28 Wyndham St, Central
Hong Kong
http://www.asia2000.com.hk/

Printed in 1999 in Hong Kong by Maison d'éditions Quaille

PREFACE

The Chinese believe the animal ruling the year in which a person is born has a profound influence on personality, saying: "This is the animal that hides in your heart."

The Chinese lunar calendar dates from 2697 BC, when the Emperor Huang Ti introduced the first cycle of the zodiac. A lunar year normally consists of 12 months, each starting on a new moon. This gives a year of about 354 days. The 11 days shortfall is made up by adding a leap month (in seven out of every 19 years). February 5th, 2000 is the first day of the Dragon year.

According to legend, the Jade Emperor was looking for 12 creatures to match the 12 years of the calendar cycle, so he held a race, which crossed a river. The cat and the rat were not good swimmers, so they rode across on the ox. Half-way across the rat pushed the cat into the water. As the ox reached the bank, the rat jumped onto the shore and raced to claim first place. The ox was second, followed by the tiger, the rabbit, the dragon, the snake, the horse, the ram, the monkey, the rooster, the dog, and the pig, and the Jade Emperor named the years in that order. The unfortunate cat didn't make the list, and this explains the hatred between cats and rats to this day.

Please see the tables at the end of this book to find the lunar year of your birthdate. You can then consult the general outlook for the year of your birth in Part I, and more detailed forecasts, for romance, business and other important topics, in Part II. Finally, the calendar of the Dragon Year advises on which activities are lucky, and which unlucky, for each day.

Good Luck!

庚辰年春牛圖

蝗蟲爲害傷田禾
年際庚辰奈若何
春夏地乾泉已竭
秋冬雨飽水嫌多

蠶娘每苦難成繭
野老偏愁枉荷簑
我相天機應有此
斯言豈必盡差訛

The locusts will swarm
destroying the plants in the field,
because this is the year of the Geng (*庚*) Dragon
In the Spring and Summer
there will be drought, cracking the earth,
even the springs will fall dry;
but in the Fall and Winter
torrents of rain will assault the earth,
and the girls tending silk worms will worry
that the cocoons will not mature;
the straw rain capes that they wear
will cause the peasants continuous sorrow;
everyone believes that fate is such,
and that this prediction shall come to pass.

CONTENTS

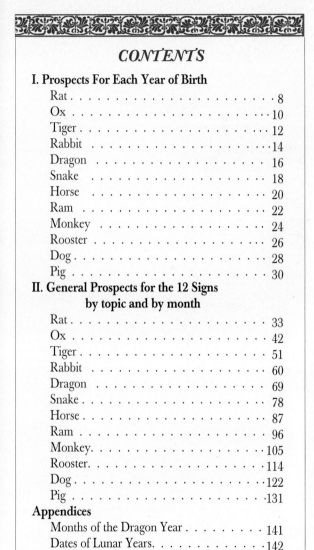

I.

Prospects For Each Year of Birth

RAT

Prospects for those born in the Year of the Rat

1912, 1924, 1936, 1948, 1960, 1972, 1984, 1996

Young people born in 1984 will find it difficult to concentrate on their studies this year; their school-work will be worse than last year. Yet they still have a thirst for knowledge. Parents and teachers must patiently guide them. Those born in 1924 are not in good health and may suffer diseases of the feet.

Those born in 1936 will have better luck than last year, yet their luck in making big money will not be so good this year. The most important thing is

family harmony. They should practice calligraphy and do gymnastics so as to keep fit.

Those born in 1948 are more successful than last year. Their luck in making money is not good in the first half of the year. They must be very cautious if they plan to invest. They have to guard against disasters and misfortunes this year.

Those born in 1960 will be very successful this year and their financial resources will be bountiful. Happy events will take place one after another, and they may bring honor to their ancestors.

Those born in 1972 will have normal luck this year. They can make a fortune in a distant land. They can make money by going out and they may have an extremely romantic love affair. Unmarried men and women might make a good match; of course they should let fate take its course, for they will not be able to force him or her to agree.

OX

Prospects for those born in the Year of the Ox

1913, 1925, 1937, 1949, 1961, 1973, 1985, 1997

Those born in 1985 are at a time of first awakening of love; they must learn to restrain themselves so as not to fail to seize the golden age. They ought to dedicate their time to studies in school and to achieving greater successes. When conditions are ripe, they may go on a long journey of discovery. Older persons born in 1925 should be even-tempered and good-humored; and the most important thing for them will to be to keep fit.

Those born in 1937 have good luck in doing business and making money, especially in the latter half of the year. But they must look after this money carefully to avoid its going quickly. Married men

and women should guard against love affairs between different generations.

Those born in 1949 are physically and mentally healthy; they have to guard against spirits and women, and try to maintain husband and wife's morale to avoid marital breakdown. As far as luck is concerned, there is half bitterness, half sweetness. If they have any chance to cooperate with others, they will need to think twice before they leap. Yet they will still have opportunities, and they should console themselves as their children will become useful persons.

Those born in 1961 are faced with acute competition and they have to be careful in meeting challenges. They will have average luck in doing business and making money. They may make rapid advances in their career. Yet they should keep away from matters of right and wrong in officialdom. Ladies should not take any bold action in dealing with love affairs.

Those born in 1973 have frequent social contacts this year. They may easily fall in love. But they have to be cautious in choosing friends so as not to fall into the trap of sexual love. They must foster lofty ideals in order to achieve great success. Their luck in earning money and making rapid career advances is good enough; they should never miss a chance when it arrives at their door.

TIGER

Prospects for those born in the Year of the Tiger

1914, 1926, 1938, 1950, 1962, 1974, 1986, 1998

School children born in 1986 will be disgruntled and will make slow progress in their studies; they must be patiently coached. They ought to be cautious when making friends. Older persons born in 1926 will be in poor health this year and they must pay attention to food hygiene.

Those born in 1938 are not so fortunate and have both good and bad luck in earning money. They work hard, but will have no gains. Moreover, they might make mistakes when discussing financial matters. Yet they are destined to find noble bene-

factors help them and they will be able to weather the storm.

Those born in 1950 will have worse luck than last year, come across lots of obstructions, and may suffer unexpected personal financial losses in the second half of the year. They must guard against mean-spirited persons, disputes, and problems with those in power. Married life is not stable for the ladies and they should not take any bold action in dealing with affairs of the heart.

Those born in 1962 may meet with lots of difficulties; their prospects will be uneven and unstable. They must avoid gambling and doing speculative business. They may find noble benefactors to assist them; money will come and go. They are romantic; they will not be able to go against their feelings.

For those born in 1974, matters pertaining to business and love will not turn out as they wish. They must deal with everything calmly and guard against impatience. They had better dedicate their energy to their studies. They should not be stubborn when seeking love; they ought to attach greater importance to their undertakings.

RABBIT

Prospects for those born in the Year of the Rabbit

1915, 1927, 1939, 1951, 1963, 1975, 1987, 1999

School children born in 1987 will do relatively poorly in their examinations. They ought to develop more hobbies and skills in extracurricular activities. They should take part in more artistic activities but not indulge in idle play. They will be in poor health and will easily catch cold. They must attach importance to food hygiene and avoid hurting their limbs. The old born in 1927 will be in poor health but they will feel much better in the second half of the year.

Those born in 1975 are very popular this year; their communication circle is greatly enlarged. They are very lucky the year round; they are successful in

business. But they may feel vexed in love affairs; their houses might be at stake and in confusion. Men should guard against the third man. Those born in 1915 are in poor health and are liable to meet with accidents; they must take special care of themselves.

Those born in 1963 have normal luck. They might be transferred to a new environment and faced with various challenges; they must seriously accept them. They should avoid gambling. They ought to learn to properly deal with matters of the family; the important thing is that men and women are on good terms. Ladies might feel vexed and the elderly will have relatively poor health.

Those born in 1951 have a good luck in business. This year suits developing outwards, but they can't treat their spouse coldly because of this and should look after each other so as not to become isolated. They must guard against accident and bloody disasters. Their brothers and friends are not favored; these people must be more careful.

Those born in 1939 will have ups and downs in making money; they must cautious of speculative business. They should never celebrate birthdays, otherwise their luck might turn for the worse. They must do exercise to keep fit. They ought to guard against diseases of the digestive system. They have good luck in traveling, but they have to pay attention to safety.

DRAGON

Prospects for those born in the Year of the Dragon

1916, 1928, 1940, 1952, 1964, 1976, 1988, 2000

Children born in 1988 will not have peace of mind this year and will feel under pressure from their studies. Their parents must show more concern for their inner world, but be careful not to spoil them. They must guard against falls and try to avoid hurting their limbs. They must try to remove misfortune, avert accidents, and keep away from bad characters for one takes on the color of one's company. Their parents ought to help them to see what is right or sensible. They will have no luck this year.

The prospects for young people born in 1976 are quite stable; their luck in making big money will be very good. But they are liable to bring trouble on themselves or get into disputes with others. Their

income will be plentiful, yet they might have unexpected financial losses in the latter half of the year. It's time for bachelors to get married; single women may get involved in triangular love affairs. They will have lots of friends. They will have luck at first and then things will change for the worse. They must understand that trouble comes out of the mind.

Friends born in 1964 may meet with one trouble after another throughout the year. They will advance despite unexpected obstructions and pressure in their work. Their fortune and luck in making money are quite good. Their married life is perfect. They are well-behaved and quick-witted. Man and woman are both in harmony. Yet they might come across resistance this year. Those born in 1952 are faced with great pressure at work; they will be physically injured and mentally affected. They must be able to endure so as to remove misfortunes and avert accidents. Fortune and luck in making money are quite good. But they might bring trouble on themselves. They should never become a guarantor in order to avoid inviting trouble. Those born in 1940 are lacking luck in making big money. They will be short of regular income and extra earnings. But their undertakings will not be at a standstill.

SNAKE

Prospects for those born in the Year of the Snake

1905, 1917, 1929, 1941, 1953, 1965, 1977, 1989

Children born in 1989 will only have average school results. They have to keep away from those with bad character. They should not play by themselves. They must guard against falls when playing. Girls will be faithful; they will enjoy a life full of peace and happiness.

Those born in 1941 will have good luck in making money, and gain profits if they invest. There will be lots of quarrels this year; they may as well save their breath. Prospects are stable. Evil characters may easily drive a wedge between husbands and wives. A casual worker might be promoted and given a raise, but must do more work. They will fret over affections and should control their sexual urges.

They will be successful in business and find many ways to make money. Those born in 1953 are sound in body and mind this year. Prospects will change for the better. Prosperity will be greater than adversity, but they had better not cooperate with relatives so as to avoid suffering losses. They must be careful to avoid breakdowns in marriage, and should guard against being tempted by evil characters. Their luck in making money begins to turn to good in the first half of the year. Wives will not feel very well in the first half of the year; they had better not be greedy; they might put on mourning dress in autumn.

Those born in 1965 may get support from noble benefactors; they may invest in a new undertaking, and they will make great plans for developing their enterprises. There is some resistance during the 5th and 6th lunar months; good fortune will be better than misfortune. But they must be very considerate to others. Females might encounter trouble in love and marriage.

Those born in 1977 may meet with trouble, but they can dispel the clouds and see the sun if they seize the right time and find a benefactor to help them. As far as love is concerned, they will have their share, but they will have no luck in finding their perfect match; it will be difficult for them to seek a sweetheart; they shouldn't be impatient for success, or they may suffer defeat when victory is within their grasp.

HORSE

Prospects for those born in the Year of the Horse

1906, 1918, 1930, 1942, 1954, 1966, 1978, 1990

During the year it will be hard for school children born in 1990 to have a breakthrough in their studies; they must be strictly supervised in order to make progress; they will be sad and depressed, so they should be helped out of goodwill. They will suffer some ailments, but nothing serious. They must be cautious not to make friends with bad characters, and guard against unexpected losses.

Those born in 1978 may meet with lots of dangers and difficulties and suffer unexpected financial losses this year; they must never be credulous as that can help avoid misunderstandings. But they will have a

change in their fortunes; their luck in making money is also good. They might have new girlfriends, but they should not take their relationships further at this time.

Those born in 1966 are confronted with change-able situations; they shouldn't act rashly and must watch for mean-spirited persons who may stab them in the back. They might seize an opportunity, but have to avoid any rash advances. Their luck in making money is quite good and they can earn money in business. The elderly born in 1906 will not be in good health this year; they must take good care of themselves. Those born in 1954 should advance gradually and consolidate at every step in their undertakings so as to avoid commercial traps. Their luck is now good, now bad. They had better not go out, and they should avoid long journeys. They must guard against falling out with their part-ner and breaking up a marriage.

Those born in 1942 will have average luck in mak-ing money this year and they had better know their place. They should be very careful when signing a contract or guarantee. Yet they can seize opportu-nities in other respects; of course they ought to think thrice before they act. In marriage life they must guard against extramarital love. They shouldn't trust friends too much otherwise they will lose vigi-lance. The 9th lunar month is the best one for those born in the year of the horse.

RAM

Prospects for those born in the Year of the Ram

1907, 1919, 1931, 1943, 1955, 1967, 1979, 1991

Children born in 1991 will be very good at thinking deeply and comprehending quickly this year, but to ensure all is well throughout the year they shouldn't be indulgent with themselves. The elderly born in 1931 will have better luck than last year.

Those born in 1943 are luckier this year than last year. Their luck in making money is sufficient and their business will boom, especially in the second half of the year. They must guard against suffering unexpected financial losses because someone in the family will fall ill.

Those born in 1955 will do their work without obstruction and will be able to makes lots of money this year, but they should not get involved in gambling or speculative business. In relationships, the most important thing is harmony.

Those born in 1967 will not only do everything successfully, but will also have luck in making money. Their lucky star will shine on high and happy events will arrive at their door. But they should be careful not to get involved in too deeply the trap of relationships.

Those born in 1979 are rich in feeling and will be able to achieve success one way or another, but they should never invite trouble. It will be no problem for them to enter a higher education or hunt for a job. They must guard against the mean-spirited; they should be cautious not to make trouble, and when they go out, they should guard against thieves.

MONKEY

Prospects for those born in the Year of the Monkey

1908, 1920, 1932, 1944, 1956, 1968, 1980, 1992

Young friends born in 1992 will find it difficult to concentrate on their studies and will be easily distracted. Though young, they might make lots of trouble; their parents have a duty to take care and educate them in order that they make good progress. Older people should take special care during the 7th and 12th lunar months; they may meet with relatively great resistance and their luck in making money is relatively bad.

Those born in 1944 might encounter twists and turns this year. They must be industrious and frugal so as to avoid suffering losses. They may have

24

trouble in financial affairs and suffer unexpected personal financial losses in the latter half of the year. They must be cautious not to be taken in because they may make mistakes in signing documents and contracts.

Those born in 1956 should not long for anything so as to avoid meeting with unexpected financial accidents. They must pay attention to the security of the house and take good care of the elderly. They must never act impetuously and have to be cautious in dealing with everything. They ought not to get involved in extramarital love, or they might suffer unexpected personal financial losses because of sexual love. Their fate trends turn for the better in the latter half of the year.

Those born in 1968 will have better luck this year than last year, but they must be moderate in all that they do. They ought to stick to their posts and guard against emotional ups and downs. Extramarital love is forbidden. Those born in 1980 will be on an emotional seesaw and they will often worry over nothing. They should never do anything foolish. Ladies will not have an easy time in dealing with affairs of the heart. Friends at school should not talk or make love; they must keep guard and strive for success.

ROOSTER

Prospects for those born in the Year of the Rooster

1909, 1921, 1933, 1945, 1957, 1969, 1981, 1993

Those born in 1993 are quick-witted and it will be the right time to go to school. Yet they are apt to lose things. They must watch what they eat as their digestive system will have problems. They are liable to hurt themselves. Prospects for those born in 1933 are quite good and luck in making money is also good.

Those born in 1945 are likely to be the envy of others and will have good luck this year. If they meet difficulties calmly, they will manage to get through. They must keep away from alcohol and the admiring looks of women.

Those born in 1957 will be extremely good at business and they will be able to find noble benefactors to guide and support them. But because they do not draw a clear distinction between public and personal interests, they will find themselves in trouble. They will easily become ensnared by women; they should never indulge themselves in lust.

Those born in 1966 may meet with difficulty in both business and feeling. They should not embark on extramarital love affairs; they may have a serious association with the opposite sex. The second half of the year is the best time to consider marriage.

Young people at school born in 1981 should develop various hobbies and skills; they might run into trouble in their studies and feelings; it's the time for gentlemen to make an offer of marriage and for fair maidens to yearn for love. But women must be cautious not to be taken in.

DOG

Prospects for those born in the Year of the Dog

1910, 1922, 1934, 1946, 1958, 1970, 1982, 1994

It's time for little friends born in 1994 to go to school. They want to make good progress in their studies. They should guard against falls.

There's nothing serious in health for those who were born in 1934, but they must be careful not to fall when going out and guard against high blood pressure and other diseases of old age. Prospects for male relatives will not be very good this year.

Prospects for those born in 1946 will be relatively poor and will get even worse in the latter half of

the year. They should remember that harmony is the way to make money. They must try to advance gradually and consolidate at every step, and to take defense as a means of offense. They should not hurt other's feelings over some trivial matter.

Those born in 1958 will find their prospects slightly improved, but on the whole there will be few advantages throughout the year. If they are lucky enough to find noble benefactors to help them all is not lost. Family life will not be harmonious; they must be cautious not to let mean-spirited persons sow the seeds of discord; they must never let themselves be seduced into ill-fated love affairs.

Those born in 1970 might enjoy success when very young. Prospects will be full of twists and turns; fortunately, there will be nothing serious. They must know that a tall tree catches the wind. Older persons born in 1910 may suffer from ailments, but they will be in a merry mood.

Young people born in 1982 may take pleasure from their emotional life, but the important thing is selecting a profession and completing their education.

PIG

Prospects for those born in the Year of the Pig

1911, 1923, 1935, 1947, 1959, 1971, 1983, 1995

Those born in 1983 tend to be relatively arrogant, rebellious, restless and whimsical. They will be resented by the people around them. Their parents should help them to see what is right or sensible. If they dedicate their energy to studies in school they will hold up their heads some day.

It's an average year for those born in 1935. Their luck in making big money will be like a flower in the fog and an image in the mirror. They should never they act rashly. They ought to avoid cigarettes and strong alcohol. There is fortune in misfortune this year; they might feel vexed in the sec-

ond half of the year; but they must be cautious not to suffer disaster and guard against illness.

Those born in 1947 might meet with lots of unexpected twists and turns. A good luck star will shine high above the ladies; and their luck in making money is quite good. They should pay attention to the health of older members of the family.

Those born in 1959 may find noble benefactors to help them, yet they will not necessarily achieve success. So they must never act rashly. In daily life, they should avoid smoking and drinking. They ought to take good care of themselves, especially their limbs.

Those born in 1971 will have good luck in the second half of the year, but the reflection in the water is not necessarily realistic. They must avoid making friends with wicked characters, or they might get involved in trouble. They have to be cautious if they are not to suffer unexpected personal financial losses. They ought to take good care of themselves.

II.

General Prospects for the 12 Signs
(by topic and by month)

RAT

LUCK

Prospects for those born in the year of the rat will not be very good throughout the year. School children born in the year of the rat may find it difficult to concentrate on their studies. In order to have a bright future they must dedicate time and energy to their schoolwork, as diligence helps remedy clumsiness.

Housewives must do their best to maintain a good relationship with their husbands, or something will go wrong with their marriage. Girls born in the year of the rat must refuse to be contaminated by men

so as to preserve their purity, otherwise a single slip may cause lasting sorrow.

They will have good luck in making money, they will not be able to earn extra money apart from their income. Thus, they ought to keep away from gambling table. Those born in the year of the rat may feel that it's difficult for them to choose a sweetheart; they ought to remember to take action according to the situation; they should never impose their own will on others if they do not want to mislead themselves or others. Their luck is quite good this year. If they go out or abroad to seek opportunities to advance themselves they will also earn extra money and other material advantages. Their prospects are not good enough; they ought to be cautious in making friends; the important thing is tolerance. Prospects turn for the better after the mid-autumn festival. They may have to wear mourning clothing within the year. If they undertake more good acts, everything will go on smoothly. Those born in the year of the rat will have a strategic mentality, but they lack a certain degree of boldness, so they often fail when they are on the verge of success. Their means of communication is not quick enough; they are relatively egotistic and often lose site of the main goal because of small gains. As their interpersonal skills are poor they will find it hard to make friends throughout their life. If they are able to overcome their shortcomings, and deal with people in a tactful manner, they will turn for the

better when reaching middle age. Girls and boys might amaze the world with a single brilliant feat; the young have average luck this year and must be cautious not to get involved in love affairs.

Their ideal matches are those born in the year of the ox and the horse.

ROMANTIC LIFE

The year 2000 is one in which males or females born in the year of the rat tend to become entangled in extramarital relationships. They will have success with others of the opposite sex.

Those born in the year of the rat would like to get married, but they do not like others giving their loved one covetous looks. Throughout the year they have a strong desire to enter into sudden romantic relationships and their emotions will be topsy-turvy. This is a year in which they had better restrain themselves; they ought to be careful in the 1st and 7th lunar months. Those born in summer are likely to act boldly; those born in other seasons must pull in their horns; those born during cold winters and in storms must be careful not to make mistakes.

Males born in the year of the rat may fall in love with several women at the same time. Males and females will both have a tendency to become involved in extramarital affairs; males will have good luck in adventures with women. Those born in the

year of the rat usually have a large family which helps to cement the relationship with the spouse.

Those born in the year of the rat should not marry those born in the year of the ram, rooster or the horse.

Marriages with those born in the year of the rabbit will not be happy.

Auspicious Colors: red, brown, yellow.
Inauspicious Colors: blue, white.
Auspicious Numbers: 1 & 8.

FORECASTS BY MONTH
1st month (February 5th to March 5th, 2000)
A month of bamboo and plum blossoms

Prospects will seem favorable but actually they are not. The time that seems favorable is not necessarily good; the time that appears unfavorable is not necessarily bad. It's a month of bamboo and plum blossoms. Those born in the year of the rat had better take defense as a means of offense; they must be cautious about everything as interpersonal relationships are complicated and prospects are inconstant. It is not the right time to start any grand plan. Their love life will be in harmony.

2nd month (March 6th to April 4th, 2000)
A month of opportunity

Prospects will be good and constant. There will be less resistance; troubles will be removed. Those born in the year of the rat will be able to find noble benefactors to guide them; females should be luckier. They will gain both fame and fortune. All is well. They ought to wait for an opportunity to stride forward. They must take good care of the middle-aged and the elderly.

3rd month (April 5th to May 3rd, 2000)
A month where things take a turn for the better

Things take a turn for the better. Though holding dinner parties is not a proper business, yet it offers an opportunity to make friends and is not a bad thing. It brings pleasure to life. They should not get involved in quarrels between friends. Middle-aged people born in the year of the rat will have luck in making money and it will be a good time to make decisions concerning investment.

4th month (May 4th to June 1st, 2000)
A month to adjust the love life

This will be a prosperous month. There will be substantial increases in income. Those born in the year of the rat had better seize the right time to purchase houses or land. To maintain favorable trends they should not visit the sick or the bereaved. During this month they are faced with a crisis in their love life. They had better treat others and ad-

just their love life calmly and properly. The most important thing is harmony. They should never assume a haughty air.

5th month (June 2nd to July 1st, 2000)
A month of yielding

This is an unlucky month and fate will take a turn for the worse. Those born in the year of the rat should yield and comply in all their dealings. They ought to show more concern for the family; husbands and wives must exercise tolerance; they have to keep away from the gambling table; they had better strictly supervise children's studies; it's important for them to be in a good mood. They must be careful so things will go smoothly.

6th month (July 2nd to July 30th, 2000)
A month to where success gradually returns

Fate will put an end to the crisis and will decree a return of prosperity. At the beginning and in the middle of the month, there will be a lot of trouble and anxiety. It is not a good time to go out. They must guard against mean-spirited persons who sow discord; if problems are handled properly, they can turn bad situations into good ones. They must take precautions against insomnia caused by nervousness and diseases of the liver and gallbladder.

7th month (July 31st to August 28th, 2000)
A month when making money will be easier

This month will be prosperous. There will be good luck in making money this month; income will be

sufficient. Males born in the year of the rat will have good luck with women; they have to learn to restrain themselves in order to avoid sexual traps; they must take good care of the aged and they might put on mourning clothing this month. They must guard against accidents and keep away from the gambling table and speculative business so as to keep money already entered into the account book.

8th month (August 29th to September 27th, 2000)
A month of good omens

A lucky star shines on high this month and the weather is clear and bright. There will be some resistance, but it is an appropriate time to act boldly and everything will be successful. Spouses or lovers will have better luck this month. Those born in the year of the rat should consult more and had better take part in things personally. They should never let down their guard as there is anxiety hidden behind good omens. It is not a good time to buy bonds and stocks or to go out.

9th month (September 28th to October 26th, 2000)
A month of ups and downs

Prospects are unsteady and full of difficulties this month; it's hard to make any progress in one's affairs. If there is an opportunity it will be the right time to fight a quick battle to achieve certain goals. It's a month for one's love life to rise rapidly and fall steeply; and the desire for sexual love is as rough as waves in the sea; it is important to tell domestic

flowers from wild flowers.

10th month (October 27th to November 25th, 2000)
A month of improvements

This month will be gradually become prosperous and things will improve. Those born in the year of the rat must be careful to manage money matters and avoid borrowing lending, investing, gambling, and traveling. They must guard against a sudden death of an elderly person. They must keep close watch over the door and take good care of old people. Their love life will be rich and colorful; they must deal with the relationships between new and old lovers and mistresses properly and be careful not to fall into sexual traps. Those born in spring must not be jealous.

11th month (November 26th to December 25th, 2000)
A month to strengthen and smooth over relationships

There are quite a lot of twists and turns this month, but one should not lose heart. Those born in the year of the rat will be able to turn bad luck into good luck; they must smooth over relationships. It is an unfavorable time to go out, yet they still will emerge safely from danger. They are full of affection, but had better keep away from sexual love and not hurt anybody just to meet their own needs. They might lose money in order to overcome their grief over failed affairs of the heart.

12th month (December 26th 2000 to January 23rd, 2001)
A lucky month

This is a lucky month. Those born in the year of the rat are very successful in business, and will have fame and wealth. They will have many sources of income. It is an unfavorable time to go out; there will be matters where they have to decide between right and wrong; they might suffer unexpected personal financial losses and mean-spirited persons may be a burden to them; they must take precautions against disease.

OX

LUCK

Those born in the year of the ox will have many obstacles in the first half of the year. They can expect a turn for the better in the latter half of the year and will have good luck in making money and starting projects. They must pay attention to love affairs because they may affect their future prospects.

The young will have great interest in the opposite sex. They will not concentrate on studies, but they should abandon them. They must try to restrain themselves and not get angry or quarrel with others.

Housewives born in the year of the ox may meet with temptations from outside and they must try to resist. They should also show more consideration for husbands so as to avoid the breakdown of their marriage. Girls born in the year of the ox will long for love; they must have penetrating insight into a person for those full of affection for a person of opposite sex might have regrets in the end. Their luck in making big money is very good, especially in the second half of the year. They have luck in investment and side gains. They may go in for overseas investment and purchase real estates.

They are active in social intercourse and are full of affection for those of the opposite sex, but they should never go overboard. Married women have a strong sexual desire and they had better avoid over-indulgence.

Business is favorable to those in cultural and educational circles. When going out they can make fortunes, but they must be cautious of accidents because many obstacles lie in their path. Disasters, misfortunes and accidents will have something to do with the opposite sex; they must avoid getting involved in sexual traps. There is some clash between one and another and obstacles follow one after another; fortunately, they are destined to have happy events arrive at their door and these will enable them to get around obstacles.

Those born in the year of the tiger, horse or ram are their best matches; those born in the year of the snake should be avoided.

ROMANTIC LIFE

In 2000 those born in the ox year will be able to handle problems in love and marriage cautiously and calmly; this year will bring a lot of money and good results, but these might also cause them to be taken in.

Troubles will cease in the 11th lunar month if they get married or take a lover. The 2nd and 6th months are the best ones for them to marry; even if this love affair is outwardly severed they will feel inwardly connected, and will treasure this relationship for life. This is a lucky year for those born in the year of the ox. Many of the opposite sex get near to those born in the ox year because they are rich. Once they find their lovers or sweethearts just love their money they will feel disappointed. Those born in the ox year will feel disappointed. Those born in the ox year are always passive and love-crossed. They are often not in a position to resist the passion or attacks of the opposite sex.

Fortunately, 2000 is luckier than the previous year. The deception played on them won't last, but it may be a great disappointment to them.

The best matches for those born in the year of the

ox are those born in the year of the rat, snake or
rooster; they should keep away from those born in
the year of the ram, dragon, horse, rabbit or dog;
the ram will overcome the ox.

Auspicious Colors: grey, blue, black.
Inauspicious Colors: green, purple.
Auspicious Numbers: 2 & 5.

FORECASTS BY MONTH

1st month (February 5th to March 5th, 2000)
A month not to ask for favors too anxiously

This is a relatively prosperous month. At the beginning of the New Year, those born in the year of
the ox will make progress in their undertakings and
gain much. But they should ask for a favor without
hesitation in order to achieve things quickly. It is a
favorable time to go out. They must distinguish
friendship from love; if they keep a distance from
close friends of the opposite sex, friendships will
last a lifetime. Precautions should be taken against
urinary disease.

2nd month (March 6th to April 4th, 2000)
A month for fortunes to decline

Those born in the year of the ox may feel as if they
are bathed in spring breezes. They might meet with
resistance; if dealt with properly, problems can be
solved easily. They will have many dinner parties

and relationships. But they must provide against danger while living in peace, set some money aside and store up in case of famine. It is not a good time to set off on a journey. They must pay attention to traffic safety.

3rd month (April 5th to May 3rd, 2000)
A month to emphasize love

Prospects may take a sudden turn and develop rapidly. However, things will be fairly steady. Those born in the year of the ox must keep vigilance; fortunately they will find noble benefactors to guide them and will make slight progress in their undertakings; they will have relatively poor luck in making money and they must guard against unexpected financial losses. Love occupies an important place this month; attractiveness lies everywhere, but sexual love affairs will not have a good end; they should never try to eat forbidden fruit. Gambling on a small scale may be relaxing, but they should not spend most of their energy and time at this pursuit.

4th month (May 4th to June 1st, 2000)
A month full of ups and downs

Life will be full of ups and downs; misfortune and good fortune are at loggerheads; gains will alternate with losses. At the beginning of the month, prospects will be fairly good; at the end of the month there will be more obstacles. Those born in the year of the ox must remember that talking too much may cause mistakes. During the month they will

have adequate income. Both males and females born in the year of the ox must be cautious not to fall into traps of a sexual nature.

5th month (June 2nd to July 1st, 2000)
A month that suits starting up

Prospects will be favorable this month, but it is not the right time to buy and sell houses or land. It is a good time to broaden one's horizons; those born in the year of the ox will always deliver on their promises. This month suits beginnings, especially westward and northwestward. On their way they may find noble benefactors to guide them. They must be cautious if they are not to suffer losses or invite trouble from officials. Married people born in the year of the ox have strong sexual appetite; they must restrain themselves. Single men and women should seize the opportunity to choose their future spouse.

6th month (July 2nd to July 30th, 2000)
A month to stay calm and pull through

This is an unlucky month, during which things will be at their lowest ebb of the whole year. Situations will suddenly change and develop rapidly. There are many matters of right and wrong that they have to deal with; there will be few opportunities for making money.

Those born in the year of the ox must be calm; they must be cautious to avoid disputes with officials. Those born in the year of the ox must be careful not to fall a prey to a plot and guard against

mean-spirited persons who strike when a person is down. Their love life will be on the verge of crisis. They must guard against intrusion by a third party.

7th month (July 31st to August 28th, 2000)
A month of hardship

There will be lots of ups and downs this month. There will be many hardships and difficulties. Those born in the year of the ox will suffer financial losses. They had better take defense as a means of offense. It's favorable to begin a new venture; they may have slight gains despite being fatigued by a journey. Their love life is in a precarious situation; the most important thing is tolerance!

They should not transfer their affections to somebody else or abandon themselves to despair. They ought to take good care of family members and themselves.

8th month (August 29th to September 27th, 2000)
A month for dawn's early light to break through

This month will be prosperous; there will be good opportunities to make money. It is the right time to broaden one's horizons, buy a house or land. Lucky signs appear at the beginning of the month; those born in the year of the ox must mind their own business. They should not quarrel with others. They must try to improve their relationships with the opposite sex, and not set foot in riotous places to find love. During the month they should avoid visiting the bereaved.

9th month (September 28th to October 26th, 2000)
A month to recover from an unfavorable position

Prospects turn for the better. Those born in the year of the ox will retrieve themselves from an unfavorable position from the past; they are proficient in doing everything and have boundless horizons opening before them; benefits will come if they work hard. It is a good time to seek their fortune in the right way and develop outward. If they take offense as a means of defense, they are bound to come out on top. Those born in the spring and summer boost the morale of others and are respected; they should be modest and prudent.

10th month (October 27th to November 25th, 2000)
A smooth and prosperous month

Prospects are good this month. Those born in the year of the ox may have windfalls; they will gain fame and wealth. It is the right time for those of a literary bent to become famous; their sexual desires will be surging high, so they must learn to preserve their purity to avoid losing all standing and reputation. Married women born in the year of the ox must resist men who flirt with them.

11th month (November 26th to December 25th, 2000)
A month to reach the peak again

Prospects will take a turn for the better this month and are full of noble aspirations. Those born in the year of the ox will work in a down-to-earth way and will be very successful if they seize opportuni-

ties as they arise. They must provide against famine and live a frugal life. They must guard against mean-spirited persons and matters of right and wrong in officialdom; the important thing is forbearance. Married women born in the year of the ox should not readily become the mistresses of other men so as not to bring disaster on the family.

12th month (December 26th, 2000 to January 23rd, 2001)
A month to plan for the coming year

How beautiful is the scene for all those born in the year of the ox. All is well; those born in the year of the ox will feel complete satisfaction in everything; financial resources will be sufficient and their good luck will hold. It's best not to go out this month; they must be cautious when doing so. They should plan well for the coming year.

TIGER

LUCK

There will be no serious problems at school for those born in the year of the tiger. But they will tend to lose concentration; they must keep away from bad people.

Housewives born in the year of the tiger should avoid building large structures in the house. They must close the door and windows to ensure safety. They must also guard against children being cut or burnt. The lasses born in the tiger year should keep away from gossips.

Their luck rises and falls when it comes to making money. They had better not invest or gamble, yet gambling on a small scale may bring relaxation and unexpected gain.

They are not in good health this year. They must pay special attention to safety and diet, and they should take precautions against infectious diseases.

They may find favor in the eyes of the opposite sex and will begin an intimate association with someone. But it will come to nothing because of gossip.

Prospects will not be so favorable because of internal and external disturbances. They will feel utterly isolated from the 4th to the 8th lunar months and must tread very carefully. Husbands and wives will often quarrel with each other; they must guard against potential enemies and crises; they should not do business with any partners; they must keep watch over theft; they should visit the sick or the bereaved.

They must adopt a steady policy. Their subordinates cause lots of trouble for them and their children, especially daughters, will show a lack of understanding; their sons and daughters should broaden their horizons. If they want to make a fortune, they'd better go in for show business or real estate, but they must be cautious of being taken in. They should buy houses or land near water and with a northern exposure. They must guard against diseases of the skin and respiratory organs.

They may find a sweetheart far away from home and things will be favorable in distant lands. But

they must guard against accidents and sexual traps, for this may be only a false display of affection that may cause family disturbances; they should lead a clean, moral life.

Suitable matches can be made with those born in the year of the rabbit or horse; they should avoid dragons at all costs.

ROMANTIC LIFE

In 2000, those born in the year of the tiger may attract the attention of the opposite sex; but they should proceed in love step by step. They will be happy this year.

Those born in the year of the tiger have strong sexual desires. They are easily excited, warm towards others and are very popular among the opposite sex. They are eloquent and sympathetic, thus making themselves hard to resist. Their love life is relatively uneventful, but spring and summer are the best seasons for them to sow the seeds of love. It's the time for those born in the year of the tiger who are married to seek extra-marital love; singles born in the year of the tiger may change lovers several times if they so desire; now separated, now reunited, but the former lovers will remain good friends. During the 7th and 12th month there is danger; they must be careful to cope with anything that may happen. Those born in the year of the tiger may get married or deal with related matters

in the 1st and 9th lunar months.

Those born in the year of the tiger are sensitive and emotional; they are good lovers, but they are too earnest. So their love life is not a very pleasant one. Females born in the year of the tiger may have many love affairs, but most won't have a happy ending.

Those born in the year of the tiger may live happily with those born in the horse or dragon year. They can happily jog along with those born in the year of the dog, but there will be both weal and woe if they marry people born in the year of the pig. They should avoid choosing partners from those born in the year of the snake or monkey.

Auspicious Colors: white, blue, green.
Inauspicious Colors: purple, black.
Auspicious Numbers: 3 & 7.

FORECASTS BY MONTH
1st month (February 5th to March 5th, 2000)
A month of bright and beautiful things

Spring comes again and everything takes on a completely new look. Those born in the year of the tiger will have good luck, especially in making money; all is well. Although a brilliant future looms, there will be latent crisis; those born in the year of the tiger must provide against danger while living in peace. It is not a suitable time to migrate or go traveling. They should not quarrel with others; they

ought to keep money and possessions in good condition; they have to seek their fortune in the right way; it is an unfavorable time to be involved in speculative business. Their love life is rich and colorful; they must be cautious not to fall into traps of a sexual nature.

2nd month (March 6th to April 4th, 2000)
A month to adjust

Prospects will be unsteady this month. Even if everything is calm, those born in the year of the tiger should never take things lightly; they must be careful not to make mistakes when preoccupied; their subordinates will want to seize power, so they should raise their guard. They ought to take care of family members, especially the elderly and take precautions against disease. When husbands and wives quarrel, the most important thing is tolerance.

3rd month (April 5th to May 3rd, 2000)
A month in the depths

Prospects will take a sudden turn for the worse; it will like being plunged into the depths of misery. There will be many restrictions on their activities.

Those born in the year of the tiger must cope calmly. They should not long for more income. They have to take precautions against disease; their health will be just so-so. They ought to guard against those contemptuous individuals who attempt to take their place. They must be content with their lot, know how to educate and guide children and have the

right way to supervise and instruct them. They should take things easy and shouldn't overwork themselves. They ought to take good care of themselves.

4th month (May 4th to June 1st, 2000)
An unsteady month

This month prospects will not be very good and may even go from bad to worse. Things will not go smoothly and many issues might be raised; financial resources will be nearly exhausted. Those born in the year of the tiger must show more concern for family members and take precautions against problems in the urinary system and sexual dysfunction.

5th month (July 2nd to June 1st, 2000)
A month to gradually advance towards success

Prospects will first decline and then flourish. There will be lots of obstacles in business, but in the middle of the month, there will be a gradual advancement toward success. Prospects will be elusive, sometimes good, sometimes bad. The important thing is forbearance. They must not act rashly and they ought to think thrice before doing anything. They may meet with trouble, but the lucky star that shines above them will mean that bad luck can be turned into their advantage.

6th month (July 2nd to July 30th, 2000)
A month when prosperity increases

Prospects are good this month; it's the right time to be eager to make progress. Some unexpected achievements, including windfalls, will occur. Those

born in 1962 and 1950 have good luck with women. Those born in 1938 might fall into love with a woman or man outside of marriage. A storm may appear out of nowhere. They must guard against sexual love affairs so as not to suffer unexpected financial difficulties.

7th month (July 31st to August 28th, 2000)
A month to await change

This month is an unlucky one. Prospects will take a sudden turn for the worse; those born in the year of the tiger will be busy at work, but they meet with lots of difficulties and their work will be in vain. They have to wait for things to change in order to get a clearer understanding of the situation. They should find some other way to earn a living and manage their financial affairs more carefully. Their friends might become enemies and husbands and wives will not be in harmony. Everything has rough edges. They must use their brains and turn enemies to friends. Those born in summer will take up a unique opportunity, have less resistance and their problems can be easily solved.

8th month (August 29th to September 27th, 2000)
A month to turn bad luck into good

Prospects will improve steadily this month. There will be some obstacles at work, but nothing serious. Luck will be much improved when making money; income will be adequate, though the opportunity is a rare one. Those born in the year of the tiger must guard against being the victim of a plot and being

betrayed by colleagues and close relatives. It will be unsuitable leave home and travel to a distant land. If they accept challenges calmly and bad luck can be turned into good luck.

9th month (September 28th to October 26th, 2000)
A month with a splendid shine

Prospects will remain bountiful this month. Those born in the year of the tiger will be able to extricate themselves from a dilemma and take much in. They may promise well and achieve victory in good order if they seize the right time to found undertakings or change a job. But they shouldn't advance rashly. They should go with the flow. They ought not to be guarantors. They might find favor in the eyes of the opposite sex. They must take good care of themselves and take precautions against diseases of the respiratory tract.

10th month (October 27th to November 25th, 2000)
A month with lasting luck

Prospects remain good this month. Those born in the year of the tiger will gain both fame and fortune. The wind has abated and the waves have calmed, yet there are still many variable factors. Luck in making big money will be good; both regular income and side income will be sufficient. They will make progress in business or studies. Their love life is rich and colorful.

11th month (November 26th to December 25th, 2000)
A month to destroy the old and establish the new

A lucky star shines this month. There will be good luck in making money; income will be sufficient, yet it will be inadvisable to overly rely on windfalls. Gambling on a small scale may be a good form of relaxation; once there is an opportunity they must take action immediately; they must devote themselves to the destruction of the old and the establishment of the new though hard work, so as to turn back the negative trends. They turn a new page in their love life, but they must be on guard against unexpected financial losses because of women.

12th month (December 26th, 2000
to January 23rd, 2001)
A month to advance cautiously

Prospects remain good this month. They will be fairly lucky in making money. There might be hidden obstacles, but they will be easy to solve if those born in the year of the tiger use their brains. But they can't act too hastily, or the gain will be no compensation for the loss. They must exercise tolerance toward their superiors. It is not a suitable time for them to cooperate with others in business or court trouble with officials. They must try to avoid being guarantors.

RABBIT

LUCK

Those born in the rabbit year will be half lucky and half unlucky throughout the year. They might change their environment and achieve promotion quickly, but to avoid rifts they should not treat their family members coldly. Young people born in the year of the rabbit may not achieve satisfactory results in examinations. They ought to cultivate many different hobbies.

The housewives born in the year of the rabbit will be in harmony with their husbands, yet they should be more tolerant and manage money matters care-

fully in summer; they had better not go on a long journey. Girls born in the year of the rabbit may make progress in looking for a sweetheart, but they must be careful not to be taken in.

Their luck in making money is rather unsteady. They must be cautious.

Their luck in earning extra income is not favorable; they ought to keep away from gambling for the time being. They are not in good health for they are always under pressure. They might enlarge their social circles and may find a sweetheart in the latter half of the year, but they should not be impatient.

They should never be careless in spending money. If they have outstanding accounts they should settle them; otherwise customers may be behind in payment and they will have bad accounts, causing cash flow to dry up.

They may find noble benefactors to assist them and it will be profitable for them to travel to distant lands. The fortune star takes its appearance this year and they should try to make money on their own initiative. They must guard against respiratory diseases and car accidents; they might suddenly fall ill.

The relationship between husband and wife will face a severe test; extramarital love will cause them much heartache. The female ought to be careful

not to invite quarrels and not to say anything off-handedly; the most important thing is harmony. Their best matches are made with those born in the year of the ram, dog or tiger.

ROMANTIC LIFE

The best wedding days for those born in the year of the rabbit are in the 2nd, 5th, 9th and 10th lunar months. They may find favor in the eyes of the opposite sex in the 1st, 6th and 11th lunar months; they might invite trouble in the 1st lunar month, and must guard against unexpected accidents in love affairs during the 6th lunar month. There might be clashes and conflicts in the 11th lunar month.

Those born in spring are the luckiest in love affairs; followed by those born in winter and autumn.

Those born in the year of the rabbit will always take the initiative in relationships. It's unsuitable for them to marry early; a late marriage may bring them a full life. If those born in the year of the rabbit and aged 36 get married this year, theirs will be a happy marriage.

All of those born in the year of the rabbit may face blows from the opposite sex and they are kinder to friends than to relatives. They must be careful in the 3rd, 6th and 11th lunar months; females born in the year of the rabbit must be cautious; the dangerous period for the male born in the year of the

rabbit is between the 3rd and 4th lunar months.

Statesmen had better select partners from females born in the year of the rabbit because although they are cautious they like showing off. Those born in the year of the rabbit are full of emotion and are always ready to help others.

Those born in the year of the rabbit appreciate artists born in the year of the ram; they can jog along with the ones born in the year of the dog or pig; they had better avoid marrying people born in the year of the rooster, rat, horse, dragon or ox.

Auspicious Colors: blue, grey, red.
Inauspicious Colors: white, orangy yellow.
Auspicious Numbers: 2 & 9.

FORECASTS BY MONTH

1st month (February 5th to March 5th, 2000)
A month during which prospects are unsteady

Prospects are rather unsteady this month; luck in making money is average. Those born in the year of the rabbit will go ahead steadily and deal surely with blows; they will be short of opportunities. They will have many sources of income, yet there will be more going out than coming in. There will be lots of quarrels with lovers. They must take good care

of themselves and take precautions against diseases of the digestive system.

2nd month (March 6th to April 4th, 2000)
A month in which obstructions lie everywhere

Those born in the year of the rabbit must cope with the situation around them with care. They must avoid stirring up trouble with officials. It will not be a good time for them to travel to a distant land and they may earn a sum of money if they seize an opportunity. They must guard against mean-spirited persons; they should never be careless; they ought to keep away from alcohol and women.

3rd month (April 5th to May 3rd, 2000)
A month when things begin to improve

Prospects take a turn for the better this month. Those born in the year of the rabbit will feel fired up with enthusiasm. Though they will have problems they will be able to solve them easily. It is a good time for them to go on a long journey to seek their fortune. They find noble benefactors to guide them; they can't become both lover and sweetheart and had better keep a distance from the opposite sex so as to keep friendships for good.

4th month (May 4th to June 1st, 2000)
A month to deal with matters calmly

Prospects will take a sudden turn for the worse and develop rapidly. Troublesome matters will come one after another, and family members and rela-

tives might become a burden. The only solution is to work in a down-to-earth way.

5th month (June 2nd to July 1st, 2000)
A month to be cautious

Prospects seem to turn for the better and everything seems to go smoothly. But it will be a sea full of submerged reefs and dangerous shoals. Those born in the year of the rabbit must be cautious about everything. They must put their accounts in order. Their family will be safe. They must keep to a light diet. Their love life will rise and fall like waves on the seashore; they should not believe in honeyed words. Females born in the year of the rabbit should not attach too much importance to romance and ought to lay stress on reality.

6th month (July 2nd to July 30th, 2000)
A month for prospects to become steadier

Prospects will become steadier this month. There is fortune in misfortune and the future is full of twists and turns. Those born in the year of the rabbit will advance despite difficulties and win victory when fate turns against them. It is not the right time to gamble. They must be cautious not to provoke trouble with bureaucracy. They ought to deal with interpersonal relationships in the proper manner. The most important thing is tolerance. They must preserve a tranquil mind.

7th month (July 31st to August 28th, 2000)
A month in which the sky clears up after the rain

Prospects will be much improved this month and there will be many noble aspirations. But those born in the year of the rabbit should still be cautious about money matters; they should not lend money recklessly. They must be careful to cooperate with others in business; they should check the accounts in person. They must be careful in daily life. They might suffer ailments once in a while, but nothing serious. Their love life is satisfactory, yet those born in 1951 must be even more careful; the most important thing is tolerance.

8th month (August 29th to September 27th, 2000)
A month with slight obstructions

This is an unlucky month. Prospects will take a turn for the worse. Luck in making money will cease. It is a bad time to invest, speculate or gamble; those born in the year of the rabbit should guard against someone who strike them while they are down. Their love life will go ahead steadily; they ought not to indulge themselves in sexual love.

9th month (September 28th to October 26th, 2000)
A month with clear and cloudless skies

Prospects will be bright. Those born in the year of the rabbit will do everything with a masterly hand;

they have luck in making big money; they win fame once again. They must seize the right time and brace themselves. They ought to be cautious about their speech and guard against arrogance and rashness. If they quarrel with friends they had better practice tolerance. Their love life will be bathed in spring breezes. Females born in the year of the rabbit must guard against intrusion from a third party.

10th month (October 27th to November 25th, 2000)
A month when everything is going smoothly

Prospects will be good this month. It is the right time to develop outwards and go overseas to seek one's fortune. But those born in the year of the rabbit must be very careful when they are out. They should bear in mind that there must be low tide after high tide. Something might go wrong with their health; they must try to improve interpersonal relationships and pay attention to the safety in the house.

11th month (November 26th to December 25th, 2000)
A month to be steady and realistic

There are reversals and twists this month; prospects will be good at the end of the month. Those born in the year of the rabbit will receive more money when they do extra work. They should work consistently and be reliable. When they achieve success they must restrain themselves. It is the right

time to go out; the best direction is northwest. They must take good care of themselves and guard against the temptations of women.

12th month (December 26th, 2000 to January 23rd, 2001) A month during which a lucky star shines

This is a month when a lucky star will shine on high. Those born in the year of the rabbit may advance rapidly in their career if they seize the right time, find suitable undertakings and lay a good foundation. It's the right time to go out and seek their fortune, but they must not neglect their love life. They must guard against mean-spirited people who make trouble; they must also keep away from matters where they must choose between right and wrong so as to greet tomorrow with a smile.

DRAGON

LUCK

Those born in the year of the dragon have little good fortune throughout the year. They must conscientiously stick to their posts so as not to be frequently taken to task. Employees had better stand fast at the post; there will not be any opportunity for them to change jobs within the year. They should never be careless in business, otherwise they may fall victims to others. They must correctly appraise the situation and draw a distinction between themselves, friends and enemies, and keep away from the rights and wrongs of a case.

For students born in the year of the Dragon, it will be no easy task to make progress in their studies. They must keep alert when taking part in extracurricular activities and guard against accidents to do with water. Housewives born in the year of the dragon might be deceived by others and so suffer unexpected financial losses. The family is in frequent turmoil. They had better be quiet instead of active. They must not act from emotion. They must be cautious of being taken in with sweet words. Things in life are complicated and confusing. They ought to know how not to be fooled, otherwise they might suffer unexpected personal financial losses and even make a wrong move.

It's the first year of a new century, and a changing year too. Those born in the year of the dragon will work well and accomplish much; they will gain fame among the people of the same trade. This year is favorable to those in the literary, art, and education worlds; they can accomplish much, and obtain both fame and material gains. The relationships between them and their subordinates will not turn for the better and many of the subordinates may leave them out. Their plans can't be fulfilled because of bad luck.

As far as luck in making big money is concerned, both regular income and side income are hard to reach their hand; obstruction often stands in the way. They must avoid gambling, investment and

speculation so as to avoid suffering unexpected personal financial losses and causing misfortune to themselves and others. They had better not visit the sick or the bereaved.

As far as health is concerned, suffering and pain will follow one after another, but fortunately nothing serious will occur. Diseases of the renal and digestive systems may occur now and then; they have to pay attention to diet, especially not to drink too much at dinner parties. There will be friction between husbands and wives leading to quarrels, and even to deadlock. They ought to deal with intimate relationships in a spirit of mutual understanding and accommodation.

ROMANTIC LIFE

The love curve seems slightly flat. The love curve starts from the 5th lunar month, but that month is full of troubles. Males born in the year of the dragon might be so absorbed in love affairs as to forget to eat and sleep and they may even commit suicide. Females born in the year of the dragon will be able to handle many suitors. They will always take the initiative in love affairs and will choose their matches carefully, but they must be cautious not to be deceived by males born in the year of the rat or to attract the opposite sex. They will have many love affairs in their life.

They always get the upper hand because they take

an indifferent attitude and are fairly aloof. They must be cautious in the 10th and 12th lunar months. There are plenty of chances for those born in the year of the dragon to be loved, but they seldom love others. Most of them do not like marrying young and many remain single all their life because they are accustomed to loneliness.

Those born in the year of the rat, monkey, tiger or rooster are good matches for those born in the year of the dragon.

Those born in the year of the dragon must avoid marrying people born in the year of the ox, rabbit, dog or dragon year.

Auspicious Colors: green, white.
Inauspicious Colors: yellow, purple.
Auspicious Numbers: 4 & 6.

FORECASTS BY MONTH
1st month (February 5th to March 5th, 2000)
A month to stand guard

They will have average luck; there's bad luck in good luck and misfortune in fortune. They must be careful not to act rashly; they must cope with challenges carefully. They should not go on a long journey in order to prevent car accidents and to avoid unexpected financial losses and injuries.

Those born in summer will have less trouble; those born in the autumn and winter must pay attention to how they use their money.

2nd month (March 6th to April 4th, 2000)
A month where things turn for the better

In this month there will be some improvement in prospects; bad luck will vanish and good luck will increase gradually; business affairs and luck in making big money turn for the better; it is a favorable time to go out. But they are liable to bring trouble on themselves with official organizations. If there are old people in the family they must take good care of them.

They must never overwork themselves and they should guard against diseases of the digestive system. Those born in the spring should do nothing but wait for their opportunity; they should never thrill to see their favorite sport and itch to have a go. Once they lose their patience, they may suffer great losses.

3rd month (April 5th to May 3rd, 2000)
A month with one climax after another

During the month those born in the year of the dragon might meet with some situations which may injure them physically and leave them mentally affected. They may find noble benefactors of the opposite sex to help them, but they should refrain from extramarital love, which might cause them to contract a disease. The unmarried may make a good

match but they must seize the right time to do so. Young people born in the year of the dragon must be careful to spend the month in a safe and secure place.

4th month (May 4th to June 1st, 2000)
A month when good fortune will break through
During the month prospects will be favorable and chances abound. But those born in the year of the dragon must be cool-headed. It is a profitable time to invest. They are liable to contract diseases and they should pay attention to their diet. Those born in the summer may find the right time to break through with a flourish.

5th month (June 2nd to July 1st, 2000)
A crucial month
During the month it will be a good time to go out, either to the south or to the north. Their prospects will take a turn for the better, but they still far from being completely good; they must still deal with all situations with care. Their luck in making money is only average. In love everything will be steady. They must guard against diseases and pay attention to health of aged members of their family.

6th month (July 2nd to July 30th)
A month to readjust and wait
During the month prospects are not very good and opportunities in making money is below average. It is an unsuitable time to expand their business; they have to take the defensive. They must lie motionless and wait. There may be trouble with those in

high places; they must be on good terms with relatives and friends.

7th month (July 31st to August 28th)
An act-with-care month

During the month prospects are stable, but those born in the year of the dragon must be prepared for sudden changes. They might meet with problems and go through all kinds of hardships to solve them. In choosing a match they must see a person clearly; they should never they be deceived by sugary words. Those born in the spring and summer must be more patient and cope with things calmly; they should never betray secrets to others because trouble may come out of the mouth.

8th month (August 29th to September 27th, 2000)
A month to have earnings

During the month prospects are stable; luck in making money is not bad. They do everything with the ease of the master. They may carry out their plans, but they can't be greedy. They will have better luck in making big money and win support from the family. But they must have penetrating insight into a person. They may go out to seek their fortune; as fortune may lie in distant lands, dinners and parties may follow one after another and their money will come and go quickly. They must guard against accidents, disasters and marriage breakdowns. But even if the opposite sex casts covetous eyes on them, they must restrain themselves.

9th month (September 28th to October 26th, 2000)
A month with abrupt changes

During the month undertakings might fall from high tide to low tide; there will be obstacles in making money. They mustn't act hastily; they should try to see the situation clearly as interpersonal relationships will be complicated; they have to keep away from wrong decisions; they ought to guard against accidents and wounds and take part in more outdoor activities to keep fit. Business will be unfavorable but love will be favorable, this is an unchangeable law throughout the ages.

10th month (October 27th to November 25th, 2000)
A month for caution

Unhappiness recedes and good luck comes; the financial situation will improve. Pay attention to market information and take extra care before signing any contracts, a mistake could cost money. They will receive help from a friend of the opposite sex, but should not get romantically involved. Take care of health, and rest more.

11th month (November 26th to December 24th, 2000)
A month to climb up the peak again

Prospects tend to be good and things will go smoothly. Yet slow progress will be made in love; they must be tolerant and distinguish good friends from bad ones. Those born in the spring and summer will have more luck.

12th month (December 26th, 2000 to January 23rd, 2001)

During the month prospects tend to rise and fall in waves. Everything will go smoothly; there will be good luck in making money. But they should never act hastily. It's unsuitable to travel to a distant land or go in for stocks and speculations this month. They had better look forward to the coming year.

SNAKE

LUCK

Those born in the year of the snake will be lucky and successful throughout the year, as they are destined to have a lucky star shine high above them. They can develop in various respects. Their aesthetic judgment will surpass others. Drawing and writing will interest them greatly. They have good luck in their old age and will lead a happy life during the days that remain to them.

Those born in the year of the snake will enjoy find others to who will support them in their fight for justice. During the 6th and 7th lunar months there

will be some slight obstruction, but everything goes on well during the rest of the months. Students born in the year of the snake will perform well; parents need not worry about their studies in school.

Housewives born in the year of the snake might put on mourning clothes in the 8th or 11th lunar months.

Girls born in the year of the snake are will feel the first awakening of love; unfortunately, they will find no one to put their trust in.

On the whole, those born in the year of the snake will have good luck this year. Their luck in making big money will be quite good; regular and extra income will come their way but they have to manage money matters carefully and remember never make ostentatious shows of wealth. Yet their luck is first good, then bad; now prosperous, now adverse. Such knotty problems as marriage breakdown, disputes or quarrels, might follow one after another.

This year is favorable to the female, but not to the male. Females will be lucky and happy events will frequently take place. Males will be unlucky and might get themselves involved in complicated and tricky affairs.

Friends born in the year of the snake are destined to provoke the almighty. They must be cautions in dealing with everything; they must guard against all kinds of unexpected losses, for no relative is willing to give them a helping hand. They ought to obey their parents and not quarrel with their elders; and not provoke those who occupy high positions. They should realize that they can avoid future sorrow if they tolerate certain situations for the time being. They should pay attention to traffic safety, drive carefully, and guard against thieves. They ought to be cautious of making new friends, and should be on good terms with gentlemen while keeping away from mean-spirited persons.

As the moon waxes and wanes this year, it will shine favorably on the female, but not to the male. Men should guard against falling into traps of a sexual nature. Those born in the year of the snake have a relaxed attitude to sexual intercourse, and will be on good terms with others; they will also have a sense of justice; they are aggressive and very much interested in art. Females born in the year of the snake are rational and often feel capricious anxiety about love and marriage. Their best matches are with those born in the year of the horse, pig or rabbit.

ROMANTIC LIFE

Males and females born in the year of the snake are attractive and have unique qualities. They always have a lot of fun with the opposite sex; they are experts in conversation and making love. But the year of 2000 is a flat one as far their love life is concerned. After all, those born in the snake year

have good luck in adventures with women. By comparison with the last year, it's a flat year.

During the 1st and 2nd lunar months new lovers turn up; the 8th lunar month is the best month for them to enjoy a passionate affair with the opposite sex; the 2nd month and 8th lunar months are the best times to get married. The 3rd lunar month will be a time of great loneliness; it's boundless torture to them. Many of them emerge from the depths of misery in the 12th lunar month. Peach blossoms of the 3rd lunar month will bring about a different situation. Those born in the spring and summer may find noble benefactors to guide them; those born in the winter must be cautious about what happens around them; those born in the autumn might need to spend money so as to restore their normal life. Around the 8th lunar month good luck in adventures with women may bring those born in the year of the snake unprecedented experience.

By and large, this is a year for those born in the year of the snake to obtain what they wish, especially in love affairs. To those born in the year of the snake who are self-confident, it will be a year when they will meet the partner of their dreams.

Their best matches are with people born in the year of the rooster; they can marry those born in the year of the ox; males born in year of the snake will tend to fall in love with females born in the year of the ox.

Those born in the year of the snake must keep away from people born in the year of the tiger and should avoid marrying those born in the year of the monkey or pig. If a male born in the year of the snake marries a female born in the year of the tiger, such a marriage may bring misfortune and disaster.

Auspicious Colors: white, grey, black.
Inauspicious Colors: green, red.
Auspicious Numbers: 5 & 8.

FORECASTS BY MONTH

1st month (February 5th to March 5th, 2000)
A month to take care

Prospects tend to be only average this month. Care must be taken in doing everything. It's relatively favorable for people to seek their fortune. Men and women will be in harmony, but have to act to prevent possible disturbance.

2nd month (March 6th to April 4th, 2000)
A month to seize the right time

During the month prospects will be fairly stable. But they still have to manage money matters with care and act cautiously. It's unfavorable for part-time workers to change to a new occupation, but when an opportunity knocks they must make a prompt decision and stand firm. When they are frustrated they had better try keep mental balance. Someone may do his or her best to help, but they

should never think themselves full of affection for a person of the opposite sex.

3rd month (April 5th to May 3rd, 2000)
A month for prospects to improve

During this month prospects will take a turn for the better. Luck in making money will be good and funds will be sufficient. One victory after another could be won, but things should be stored away in order to avoid famine. If alternative income is sought, many may suffer unexpected financial losses. There might be trouble arising out of love affairs, but they should be nothing serious.

4th month (May 4th to June 1st, 2000)
A month to ascend

During the month prospects remain good; there will be many financial resources; both fame and fortune will arrive. It's favorable to seek fame and wealth in a distant land, but there will be obstacles; special attention must be paid to speech for trouble often comes out of the mouth.

5th month (June 2nd to July 1st, 2000)
A successful month

During this month prospects are still good. Those born in the year of the snake may try their best to earn money and dip into stocks and investment. They may find noble benefactors assist them, but they have to tell love from friendship and seize the right time to make money. Those born in the winter of the year of the snake can never think themselves

full of affection for a person of the opposite sex.

6th month (July 2nd to July 30th, 2000)
A month of sudden turnings

Prospects will begin to weaken and even suffer a drastic fall this month. Luck in making money changes for the worse; it would be unwise to invest further. Noble benefactors might be found to assist them to get through a crisis. They had better be on the defensive and refrain from speaking ill of people. To maintain their mental balance they should practice relaxation and cultivate a kind heart and the love of nature. It will be unwise to go on a business trip during this month.

7th month (July 31st to August 28th, 2000)
A month to greet the sunshine

During the month prospects will be gloomy. Those born in the year of the snake should be patient, so that problems might be solved step by step. They must be confident despite the darkness before dawn. They should be careful not to fall into traps of a sexual nature. Those born in the winter of the year of the snake should restrain themselves and seek an opportunity to promote themselves.

8th month (August 29th to September 27th)
A bright month

This is a month when prosperity will arrive. Those born in the year of the snake will be free of the ill

wind of the last two months and will be filled with pride and elation.

Things will go on more or less fairly steadily and any remaining problems will eventually be solved. But sexual traps exist everywhere; they had better act cautiously and attach more importance to their undertakings.

9th month (September 28th to October 26th, 2000) A month full of power and grandeur

During this month those born in the year of the snake will be destined by fate to live under a lucky star. Their prospects will be full of power and grandeur. Females born in the year of the snake will have many challenges, but they must prevent against miscalculations and seize the right time to advance themselves.

10th month (October 27th to November 25th, 2000) An undulating month

During the month fate trends tend to be up and down. Those born in the year snake must consolidate at every step; they should not overly trust relatives and friends and they should think independently; they must pay attention to the safety of the house and avoid unexpected misfortune. Some will be lucky and some less lucky; those born in the spring of the year of the snake may turn bad luck into good, but those born in the summer of the year of the snake might put on mourning clothing.

11th month (November 26th to December 25th, 2000)
A month to fulfill oneself

A prosperous month; both regular income and side income are sufficient. From the beginning of the month, prospects tend to be stable and remain lucky in the following two months. It's a suitable time to travel to distant lands and make advances. But they should not get involved in disputes and should drive carefully. They might have good luck in adventures with a woman, but never should they let themselves indulge in such temptation.

12th month (December 26th, 2000
to January 23rd, 2001)
A prosperous month

During this month everything will go well; fate and luck in making money will be good; meanwhile there are noble benefactors to support them, and their undertakings are flourishing. Those born in the spring of the snake year must prevent against unexpected blows, those born in the summer of the year of the snake may get unexpected support, while gains and losses may cancel each other out.

HORSE

LUCK

Those born in the year of the horse will have indifferent health. They might meet with knotty problems, but they will be able to solve them. They will also achieve good results in their examinations and may even become the most successful candidates. If they work hard, they will win great victories.

Women born in the year of the horse will are indifferent in marriage life. They must try to maintain a good relationship with their husbands in time and promote mutual understanding and accommodation. Otherwise things will go from bad to worse.

Loose tongues will cost them dearly this year.

Girls born in the year of the horse should not believe everything that they are told. If they do, misunderstandings and breakup may occur. Those born in this year will dare to run risks and are quick-witted. Interpersonal relationships are good. Thus they may find noble benefactors assist them and will well be on the road to success.

Those born in the year of the horse will be luckier in the latter half than in the first half of the year; they will be pestered beyond endurance, and have good luck in adventures with the opposite sex. The married ought to be cautious of falling into traps of a sexual nature; the unmarried may hear wedding bells. The 9th, 10th, and 11th months are the best days to get married.

Those born in the year of the horse may meet with trouble and will become involved in disputes with officials. Cooperation with others or mediation for others is unsuitable. If not careful, a storm may appear out of nowhere and they may invite trouble to themselves. They may find noble benefactors help them and achieve considerable achievements in business. If they fall into traps of a sexual nature, they might suffer heavy losses. They make suitable matches with those born in the year of the rabbit, snake and dog; they can happily fool around with those born in the year of the ox, but as a couple they might fight all the time. Females born in the

year of the rabbit are willful, but they have delicate and charming features and enjoy good fortune and handsome salaries.

ROMANTIC LIFE

To those born in the year of the horse, this year is full of susceptibility and conflicts. Therefore, there might be many love affairs during the year. Males born in the year of the horse may find their sweethearts in the spring; in the 5th lunar month their relationships will be on the verge of breakup. Females born in the year of the horse will have lots of chances to enjoy sexual love in the middle of spring, summer and autumn and early winter, but at the end of each season they may get a divorce. Those born in the year of the horse are the weak in love. Tricks are often played on them. The year of 2000 sees a bumper harvest in love, but they may be disappointed and heartbroken. Spring is the right time for them to get married; the 9th lunar month is the best time for a wedding.

Young people born in the year of the horse will feel that the year of 2000 is both calm and happy; middle-aged people born in the year of the horse feel that they will be too involved in love affairs, which might bear unhappy fruit. 2000 is a year for those born in the year of the horse to meet their heart's desire in choosing matches. They love being active, and are frank when they seek love, but they hate simplicity and directness. As they know

exactly what to love and what to hate, most females will marry late; only can those born in the rabbit, snake or dog year will dally with them.

Those born in the year of the horse can live happily with people born in the year of ram and can get along with those born in the year of the dog or tiger.

Those born in the year of the horse can't marry people born in the rat, ox or rabbit years.

Auspicious Colors: green, grey.
Inauspicious Colors: white, orangy yellow.
Auspicious Numbers: 4 & 9.

FORECASTS BY MONTH
1st month (February 5th to March 5th, 2000)
A month in which a golden opportunity arrives
During the month there will be an opportunity to advance, but those born in the year of the horse should not be so impatient for success. Money comes and money goes; in fact their luck in making money is low; they have more fame than wealth. They will be on good terms with relatives; they should not go out; they must be cautious of making friends so as to avoid falling a prey to a plot.

2nd month (March 6th to April 4th, 2000)
A month to advance smoothly
Prospects are good, but those born in the year of the horse must not act recklessly when investing.

This month is better than last month, but they still face distant and imminent danger. During the month they may find noble benefactors to support them; males are likely to have an opportunity to develop their business.

3rd month (April 5th to May 3rd, 2000)
A month with half good luck and half ill luck

During the month prospects will be half lucky and half unlucky. At the beginning of the month things will go on smoothly, but in the middle of the month prospects will turn sluggish. There are many obstacles when those born in the year of the horse are out. They must keep watch in case ill luck causes losses. They may wait for noble benefactors' arrival and be able to turn their luck around. There will be more chances for those born in the summer of the year of the horse than ones born in the winter.

4th month (May 4th to June 1st, 2000)
A month to accomplish one's goal

During this month prospects will be full of twists and turns. Money matters must be carefully managed so as to reduce losses; it's an unsuitable time for any windfalls. Those born in the horse year must wait and seize the right time; they might rush about this month to solve problems, but they have to conduct themselves calmly in society. They must guard against the rivals of the opposite sex and can never let down their guard.

5th month (June 2nd to July 1st, 2000)
A month to complete important tasks

During the month there will be the unfavorable and the favorable; there is not much improvement in prospects. When business is under unfavorable circumstances, those born in the year of the snake must submit to humiliation in order to complete important jobs; they should not avoid conflict so as to avoid losses. They have to be cautious in doing business and keep away from evil characters. Noble benefactors will appear and guide them, so they will be able to dispel the dark clouds, draw the veil from the sun and restore justice. They ought to guard against sex traps; those born on the first day in the year of the snake must take care.

6th month (July 2nd to July 30th, 2000)
A month to conserve one's strength

At the beginning of the month things are not yet flourishing; the success dawns and income will increase gradually. After the middle of the month everything will be all right. Young people born in the year of the horse will make good progress in their studies; the middle-aged born in the year of the horse will lead a harmonious life; the elderly born in the year of the horse will be in good health.

Things will go well and everyone should look forward to a more beautiful future. Gambling is under a ban; investment in risky business should be avoided.

7th month (July 31st to August 28th, 2000)
A month marked by happy days

Prospects will be very good; everything is done with a master's hand; the god of wealth does them a special favor. Considerable returns can be got in stocks and finances. Once the time is mature those born in the year of the horse will get what they deserve. Regular income and extra income will be sufficient, but they should not be beside themselves with pride. In dealing with domestic issues, big issues should be turned into small ones and small ones into nothing. Elderly people born in the year of the horse should not be stubborn and ought to heed what others have to say.

8th month (August 29th to September 27th, 2000)
A month to be careful in romance

Prospects remain good, even better than last month; those born in the year of the horse will gain fame, fortune, and many other advantages. Financial resources will be sufficient if they do not pursue lofty goals. But they should not be lavish with their money or as greedy as a wolf. To take liberties with and seduce a woman risks an evil fate.

9th month (September 28th to October 26th, 2000)
A safe and secure month

Prospects tend to be average and steady in the main. There are many chances, and a lot of twists and turns. Those born in the year of the horse will be faced with challenges at work. They will make ap-

propriate arrangements and cope with matters properly. Those born in 1942 will have good luck this month and gain both fame and fortune. Neither husband nor wife should treat the other party coldly; they should never be credulous so as to avoid being used by others.

10th month (October 27th to November 25th, 2000)
A month with setbacks

This month is an unlucky one. Prospects are unfavorable and there will be twists and turns. Those born in the year of the horse must check accounts and sign documents with care; they must keep away from rights and wrongs in the officialdom. They may suffer unexpected personal financial losses at the end of the month. They must practice temperance in sexual love; if they fall in love with a married woman, it may cause quarrels between husband and wife and may sew the seeds of even more serious problems. Those born in the winter of the year of the horse will have less trouble; those born in the summer of the year of the horse will be able to face a situation at ease.

11th month (November 26th to December 25, 2000)
A month where things take a turn for the better

Prospects will improve. Those born in the year of the horse may find fulfillment and many may receive a windfall. They can turn ill luck into good as noble benefactors will support them; they ought to deal with the relationships between the opposite sex

properly so as to avoid trouble; they should pay attention to health, especially the respiratory tract. Those born in the summer and autumn will shine step by step.

12th month (December 26th 2000 to January 23rd, 2001)
A month to think before speaking

Those born at the beginning and end of the year of the horse will not be very lucky. Those born in the horse year are very talkative; they have to pull in their horns this month and deliver speeches that have been carefully thought out. The year is approaching its end and they must manage money matters and personnel affairs properly. It's unfavorable for them to travel to a distant land. There are turns and zigzags in choosing a match. They must take good care of themselves. Older people born in the year of the horse should look at the world dispassionately so that they can lead a happy life and make their old age a golden time.

RAM

LUCK

Those born in the year of the ram will be very successful this year, especially in the first half of the year.

Children and young people born in the year of the ram are good at thinking deeply and judging wisely; they will absorb various kinds of knowledge very easily. If their parents can give them friendly guidance, their talent in studies in school will show itself. But they have a tendency to tell lies; they should try to rid themselves of such a bad habit. House-

wives born in the ram year will be on good terms with their husbands; even when there is a quarrel they can revive old friendships. One happy event may follow another in the family. They are faced with so many potential marriage partners that they may not know how to choose between them.

Those born in the year of the ram will have a regular income; in the first half of the year they may also have extra income, but they must stop before going beyond the limit so as to preserve results already achieved. They will profit by their investment in the latter half of the year, but they should not long too hard for extra income.

As far as love is concerned, those born in the year of the ram may feel that both sides have advantages and will not know what course to take. They must make a reasonable choice so as not to mislead themselves and others. They are luckier this year than last year, but they will still be under pressure with many obstacles in their path. Their emotional life will be rich and colorful, but it's a year when their marriage will be tested.

Friends born in the year of the ram will find it hard to avoid affection from the opposite sex, and romantic affairs may follow one after another; they the initial excitement at the beginning so such a fate seems to be irresistible.

Quarrels and disputes might arise between friends and relatives. They must guard against discord in the home and lawsuits among relatives, as even the heavenly bodies will line up against them at this time. They must keep watch over any signs that their relatives may depart this world, as the star in charge of mourning clothes will be rampant at this time. They ought to pay special attention to safety of family members, especially the aged. This year they will have money reserves which they should keep in a safe place, for fear of loss.

Those born in the year of the ram will be lucky throughout the year. Young men and women should seize the right time to get married. In business they may find noble benefactors assist them and there will be full scope for their abilities. If they follow a down-to-earth style of work, they may achieve great benefit. They have may have the opportunity of going on a long journey; no matter whether it is a public or private trip, they would have satisfactory gains. Within the year happy events will often arrive at their door and everything will run smoothly. They should take good care of themselves and guard against epidemic diseases, especially when they are out; they never should be reluctant to leave public places where alcohol and women are concerned. They should go home as early as possible when attending dinner parties in the 1st and 3rd lunar months so as to turn ill luck into good. The best matches are with those born in the year of the mon-

key, rooster and ox; they must avoid marrying the people born in the year of the tiger.

ROMANTIC LIFE

Those born in the year of the ram will reach the peak of their love fortune between summer and autumn; the 5th lunar month is the best month. In the year 2000 they will have good luck in adventures with the opposite sex.

Males born in 1943 ought to be cautious not to commit adultery in the 7th lunar month so as to avoid quarrels and disputes. The best months to make love are the 1st, 5th, 6th, 10th and 11th lunar months. Summer is the best season to hold a wedding. Love affairs may invite quarrels and disputes, love and enmity, in the 10th and 11th lunar months; this kind of love is not pleasant, but the possibility for it to be a great one makes those born in the year of the ram the most soul-stirring amongst the 12 animals.

Females born in the year of the ram attach great importance to safety. Girls born in the year of the ram often dream of their marrying a wealthy man; they may become famous women, prostitutes, social-butterflies, advisors, public relations ladies, or even great artists or writers. Those born in the year of the ram may have lots of long-lasting love affairs and they will often get excited.

Those born in the year of the ram may live happily with people born in the rabbit, pig or horse year.

They should avoid marrying those born in the rat, ox or dog, or they will work hard all their life and their marriages won't last.

Auspicious Colors: yellow, green.
Inauspicious Colors: white, black.
Auspicious Numbers: 1 & 5.

FORECASTS BY MONTH
1st month (February 5th to March 5th, 2000)
A month with a good beginning

Those born in the year of the ram will wipe away the haze of last year. At the beginning of spring everything is plain sailing and happy events will arrive in a steady stream; luck in making money will be good. But they must be cautious of signing documents and borrowing or leading money; they should not have extramarital affairs. It is not a suitable time to go on a long journey. They might suffer ailments, but they will be nothing serious; if they are optimistic their ailments will disappear.

2nd month (March 6th to April 4th, 2000)
A month to leap ahead

During the month, a lucky star will shine high above. Noble benefactors will lend a helping hand. Business will boom. Making money and seeking wealth is good, because this wealth comes from the north. If those born in the year of the ram sit an exam, they will show their talent. When going out

they must guard against accidents. Sexual desire will surge this month, but they must restrain themselves. Those born in autumn and winter in the year of the ram must avoid accidents, should not visit the bereaved, and ought to keep away from dangerous situations.

3rd month (April 5th to May 3rd, 2000)
A month to develop undertakings steadily

During the month, business will develop steadily. Those born in the year of the ram will try to be low-key at work; they will have little luck in making money, so they had better lower their horizons. Their spouse may be the one that helps them the most. They must mind their own business and try to avoid disputes. In doing business they might cooperate with the opposite sex, but must be careful not to fall into sexual traps.

4th month (May 4th to June 1st, 2000)
A month to be steadfast and persevering

Prospects are wonderful during the month. Everything is plain sailing; business is booming; the chances of making money will be good. Those born in the year of the ram must avoid relatives and friends who demand too much; they should guard against clashes between them and their colleagues. They will overextend themselves, so they must take good care of their individual needs. They ought to be patient and tolerant. Someone may offer help, but they should not ask for too much.

5th month (2nd June to July 1st, 2000)
A month full of good opportunities

Prospects will be average; it's high time to get one's act together and consider finding a new job. Those born in the year of the ram should think twice before they act; they shouldn't be conceited or contemptuous. Females feel the need for love this month, but they must be careful not let mean-spirited persons sow discord when choosing a partner.

6th month (July 2nd to July 30th, 2000)
A month to climb up to the peak again

During the month prospects will improve; it is time to climb up to the peak again and gain both fame and wealth; mean-spirited persons and extramarital affairs must be guarded against. Those born in year of the ram can't overindulge themselves and they must constantly be on their guard. Those born in summer and winter of the year of the ram will each have their own good luck.

7th month (July 31st to August 28th, 2000)
A month to accept a challenge with composure

Prospects are average; but luck in making lots of money will be good. Regular income will be sufficient for all needs and it will be profitable to invest. Health will improve. There will be pressure and resistance at work; those born in the year of the ram must accept any challenge with composure; they will find fame, but they must guard against bad reputation through relationships with women. Those born in 1955 will have peace of mind.

8th month (August 29th to September 27th, 2000)
A month to provide against danger

During the month a lucky star shines on high and happy events will arrive at the door; noble benefactors will be met; it is a good time to go out and establish oneself in a new environment. It will be necessary to accumulate things as insurance against famine and to provide protection against danger while living in peace. They must also guard against extramarital love affairs.

9th month (September 28th to October 26th, 2000)
A month to do everything with care

Prospects tend to be rather static, but signs that things will decline further will already be visible. Those born in the year of the ram must be all the more careful to retain good luck. They must think twice before they invest so as to avoid unexpected financial losses. The house is safe and secure; domestic life is peaceful. It's the right time for those born in 1967 to get married.

10th month (October 27th to November 25th, 2000)
A month of low spirits

During the month young people born in the year of the ram will be in low spirits, as their luck in the latter half of the year will not be as good as in the first half of the year. They may travel to a distant place for relaxation and they might have unexpected gains. They must prevent against commercial traps during the month; they must never take the enemy

lightly so they can put themselves in an invincible position.

11th month (November 26th to December 25th, 2000)
A month of decline

Prospects will suffer a drastic decline this month. There will be twists and turns in work; those born in the year of the ram must cope with the situation calmly so as to reverse these negative trends; they should avoid extramarital affairs and prevent themselves becoming too involved if they don't. They must guard against disasters and work diligently in order to overcome crises.

12th month (December 26th 2000
to January 23rd, 2001)
A month to conceal one's capacities

Everything will continue on its merry way, but prospects will begin to decline. Those born in the year of the ram must know there are more dangers when one is in a high position. They must be frank and sincere with their colleagues. A harmonious relationship will bring fortune, and suffering losses is happiness. It will not be easy for one to be frank and sincere.

MONKEY

LUCK

There will be a lot of twists and turns for those born in the year of the monkey. They have to run about this year and they will meet with lots of trouble on the way. It's difficult for them to concentrate on their studies; this may seriously affect their examination results.

Housewives born in the year of the monkey are liable to fall ill. Girls born in the year of the monkey will feel the indifference of those around them and sigh for they have no close friends; they should guard against evil characters. Those born in the year

105

of the monkey will not have much regular or extra income; they should avoid investment and gambling. They ought to pay attention to their health, especially in the 8th and 12th lunar months.

This year good luck and ill luck will be mixed together. It will be both advantageous and disadvantageous. Those born in the year of the monkey should be careful in all their activities. Generally speaking, they must be patient and persevere in their attempts to increase their income; they will finally achieve success. They must guard against potential disasters and tumors. When they go out they should drive carefully.

They will feel greatly vexed; they might engage in extramarital love with a woman, for instance, living together or hiding a delicate and charming mistress. Ladies will be greatly attracted towards the opposite sex and will be eager to find a sweetheart; they might meet with a lover who is older than they are. Unfortunately, three ill-luck stars will each take their turn, so those born in the year of the monkey must be cautious when making friends. There is more bad luck than good luck this year. The best matches will be those who are born in the year of the dragon, rat or tiger year. Some may sit with their children on their knees.

ROMANTIC LIFE

The year 2000 is not pleasant since sexual love will leave only trouble and agony.

Those born in the year of the monkey tend to fall in love easily. They cast off lovers just as easily and are on constant lookout for new ones.

The 4th, 6th and 10th lunar months are likely times for those born in the year of the monkey to shift love from one to another. They can easily fall into the snares of love. In 2000, they will feel little need for love and they might think it nonessential. In winter, their fortunes will be at a low ebb and they will find it necessary to seek comfort from the opposite sex. Autumn is a good season for them to hold a wedding party; the best time for a marriage is in the 9th or 10th lunar month.

Those born in the year of the monkey can handle love affairs with great finesse and may part with the opposite sex quite cheerfully. These are their innate qualities. This is what the other animals want to learn but can't pick up. Though romantic, they are not on good terms with the opposite sex and their love life is not a happy one.

Those born in the year of the monkey will get along well with the people born in the year of the rat or dragon. They should avoid marrying those born in the year of the tiger, snake or pig.

Auspicious Colors: white, blue, black.
Inauspicious Colors: brown, yellow.
Auspicious Numbers: 2 & 6.

FORECASTS BY MONTH
1st month (February 5th to March 5th, 2000)
A month of slow prospects

This month is unlucky, the most sluggish of the year.

Those born in the year of the monkey must take defense as a means of offense, and withdrawal as a means of advancement. In unexpected misfortune they must act according to the changing situation. There will be twists and turns in choosing a marriage partner; they must be patient; it will not be not necessary for them to be stubborn; they must prevent against attacks by all possible means and they should know a true man never stands at a danger zone. When they are frustrated they had better take things calmly.

2nd month (March 6th to April 4th, 2000)
A month for dawn's early light to show itself

Prospects remain steady this month, but there will be twists and turns; those born in the year of the monkey must manage money matters carefully; it will be unsuitable for them to invest and gamble. There will be obstacles in business, but they will meet with success in love and receive some conso-

lation. In greeting the light of early dawn, they might meet with such accidents as falls and so suffer injury.

3rd month (April 5th to May 3rd, 2000)
A month to take precautions against sex traps

Prospects will take a turn for the better; those born in the year of the monkey must seize the right time and go along with the tide, but they must able to make best of noble benefactors' help and bring it into full play. It is not a good time to go traveling. They should lead a quiet life and take defense as a means of offense. Extramarital affairs will distract them and they must try to resist them in order to maintain peace within the family. Those born in spring will see their reputation enhanced; those born in autumn should try to see the situation clearly and adopt an appropriate policy.

4th month (May 4th to June 1st, 2000)
A misfortune-reaches-the-limit month

There is much improvement in prospects this month, during which misfortune reaches its limit. Those born in the monkey year are filled with pride and elation; their luck in making big money is good and their income will be sufficient. But their prospects will be unstable and others are apt to pick holes in what they have done. They must avoid extramarital affairs and be cautious when making friends. They should guard against gossip and take things calmly. They must remember the saying that joy at its height engenders sorrow.

5th month (June 2nd to July 1st, 2000)
A month to take good care of oneself

Prospects will ebb and flow. There is not anything good to say.

Those born in the year of the monkey should not act hastily for the time being. There will be internal and external obstructions and it will be hard to earn money; they will have to earn more income and cut down on expenditure. They must be cautious of speech and actions. They ought to keep away from situations where they have to choose between right and wrong; the most important thing is tolerance. It is an unsuitable time to visit the bereaved. They must take good care of themselves and go a diet. It will be extremely important to keep fit.

6th month (July 2nd to July 30th, 2000)
An overcast and stagnant month

Prospects this month will be slightly better than last month. But those born in the year of the monkey will have storm clouds hovering over business affairs and affairs of the heart. They must guard against relatives and friends' interference in their decisions. There family will not be peaceful; they should avoid sex traps when going out. They might invite rights and wrongs in the officialdom. They must be careful about everything when they go out. Those born in spring and summer will have fewer twists and turns; those born in autumn and winter can also reach their goal through their own efforts.

7th month (July 31st to August 28th, 2000)
A daring-to-make-progress month

Prospects will improve this month. Those born in the year of the monkey may find noble benefactors to support them, help them in their undertakings and they will be daring in their attempts to make progress. Their luck in making money will be first decline and then rise; in the middle of the month there will be improvement. They might quarrel with their partners and that could lead to breakup. They must be cautious about whether they are right or wrong when they deal with officials. They should behave properly in matters relating to sexual love and they should take good care of themselves.

Those born in summer will be the happiest ones this month.

8th month (August 29th to September 27th, 2000)
A month to keep a sharp lookout

Prospects will not be good this month, but there will be plenty of chances. Those born in the year of the monkey must be careful to tell the real from the false. They have to keep a sharp lookout and can't be over-anxious to get quick results and instant benefits. They ought to prevent against sex traps, quarrels and unexpected losses.

9th month (September 28th to October 26th, 2000)
A month for the lucky star to take its turn

During the month a lucky star will shine on high. Problems in business can readily be solved. But it's

unsuitable to be a guarantor; only after reading carefully should documents and contracts be signed. Mutual understanding and accommodation in love will help to get through crises. It's a month for those born in the year of the monkey to turn ill luck into good.

Those born in summer are the luckiest ones; happiness will be extremely easy to obtain. The middle-aged have luck in love.

10th month (October 27th to November 25th, 2000)
A month where hope is on the horizon

Prospects will be overcast and stagnant. But there is a good omen that things will take a turn for the better. Everything will go on well if things are undertaken step by step; then ill luck can be turned into good luck. When going out, those born in the year of the monkey may find romance. But they must prevent against potential disasters.

11th month (November 26th to December 25th, 2000)
A specious month

Prospects will be complicated and confusing, and seem to be false but in fact true. If prospects did not change for the better last month, this month will be much better. Those born in the year of the monkey may go on a long journey and can make their fortune and have romance as well. But they had better not indulge themselves in alcohol and women and should have self-respect. Those born in the year of the monkey will gain fame with each passing day, but they must be cautious about troublesome matters.

12th month (December 26th 2000
to January 23rd, 2001)
A month to take precautions

Prospects are both on the rise and on the decline. Those born in the year of the monkey must be patient and take a prudent attitude; they must be cautious about speech and actions. They must be on guard not to make any mistakes; they must avoid accidents. If they get through difficulties and hardships things will improve greatly.

ROOSTER

LUCK

Prospects for those born in the year of the rooster take a turn for the better this year. They will be proficient in money matters and doing business. With the help of noble benefactors they might rise steeply, but they will fall prey to the envy of others; they must be cautious of traps laid by others. They ought to deal with interpersonal relations carefully. They are destined by fate to have many a lucky star shine above them; it's the right time for them to unfold their grand plan and they should not miss this opportunity. Businessmen have to make progress this year; their luck in making big

money is quite good. Those who seek their fortunes must first undergo much suffering; the more difficulties they come across, the more abundant their rewards will be. They might meet with twists and turns and they may face conflicts with those of the opposite sex. Their children might put them in an awkward situations if conflicts break out over trivial matters. Unmarried people who are passionately in love may look forward to a happy marriage.

They must keep secret in doing things in case mean-spirited persons spy on them and steal the secrets of their success. They might meet with quarrels or disputes and suffer some ailments; they should guard against these, but they will be nothing serious. Those born in the year of the rooster must avoid working high above the ground within the year so as not to worry about a fall.

Good will be rewarded with good. Those who do good deeds will only have to pay attention to their diet in their later years. Those born in the year of the rooster are mild and kind-hearted, and attach great importance to friendship; they are always ready to spend money and energy in order to maintain a friendship. Those born in the year of the rooster will have a relatively strong sexual desire; but they must be cautious of not inviting misfortune because of this. They are liable to miss an opportunity when it presents itself. They have a strong aesthetic sense and a good memory. They will meet

people who will become good friends. Females will be full of wisdom, chaste and undefiled. Their best matches will be with those born in the year of the ram, pig, ox or snake.

ROMANTIC LIFE

2000 is a year full of changes and uncertainties for those born in the year of the rooster. They ardently love the opposite sex. The 1st lunar month is one where they will bring their interests into play; the 3rd to the 4th lunar months are the best time for them to gallop across the field of love; the 6th and 12th lunar months are the right time for them to show off. The biggest crisis in love comes during the 9th month, when others will dislike them and lovers desert them. They often hurt themselves in order to help the ones they love. They often disappoint lovers for they are unable to keep their promises. But they have their merits; their actions arise out of sincerity and good intentions.

Males born in the year of the rooster are often on the prowl among groups of females; they are fond of showing off, but they do not go too far and won't act recklessly without paying attention to propriety; yet the opposite sex might dislike them.

Those born in the year of the rooster get along well with people born in the year of the ox, dragon or snake, but they must try to avoid marrying those born in the year of the rat, rabbit, rooster or dog.

Auspicious Colors: red, purple, pink.
Inauspicious Colors: grey, black.
Auspicious Numbers: 3 & 8.

FORECASTS BY MONTH
1st month (February 5th to March 5th, 2000)
A promising month

Spring awakens and all things appear fresh and gay. Prospects for those born in the year of the rooster will be good. Though they run risks, they have noble benefactors to guide them; they will feel shocked over a matter but it will not be dangerous. It's favorable to go traveling and wealth lies in a distant place. They are a premonition of bright prospects for the New Year.

2nd month (March 6th to April 4th, 2000)
A month to be on guard

This month is an unlucky one. Prospects will be unsteady. Those born in the year of the rooster must be on their guard. They are not afraid to be innovators; when in difficulty, they will have noble benefactors to support them and will manage to get through. They must be careful not to make mistakes or to be taken in and they shouldn't let down their guard. And they ought to take good care of the elderly in the family.

3rd month (April 5th to May 3rd, 2000)
A month of much improvement in all respects

Prospects will be good this month. Those born in the year of the rooster will be in their glory and full of noble aspirations. A lucky star will shine on high; they will be elated at the arrival of spring and have noble benefactors to support them; there will be much improvement in making money; and noble benefactors of the opposite sex will help them out. But they should never fall in love with business contacts. Those born in spring and summer will have sudden burst of good luck, which will help them to achieve their goal.

4th month (May 4th to June 1st, 2000)
An annoying month

Prospects will be relatively poor this month. Those born in the year of the rooster often meet with obstruction in their business affairs. They must make ready for the attack. They have to guard against discord sowed by others, or they might invite troubles with officials. They behave disgracefully in sexual intercourse; they are in poor health; they will often have toothache and stomachache.

5th month (June 2nd to July 1st, 2000)
A month to become more and more prosperous

Prospects will become more and more favorable. Those born in the year of the rooster will have good luck in both business and money; they will have noble benefactors to assist them; their professional

work will be free from obstruction. They may travel to a distant land this month. They must prevent stomachache and may have to see a doctor, but the problem will not be severe. They ought to guard against unfaithful friends.

6th month (July 2nd to July 30th, 2000)
A lucky month

There are many lucky stars shining high above. Prospects are good and all is well. The family is in harmony; everybody is in good health; luster is added to the family; it's favorable to go out; there are noble benefactors to support them; luck in making money is good; there will be a breakthrough in love affairs and there will be the possibility of marriage. But they must guard against accidents.

7th month (July 31st to July 28th, 2000)
A month better for the female than the male

Prospects are on the decline this month; luck in making money will not be good. Those born in the year of the rooster must manage money matters carefully. They may find noble benefactors support them when they meet with obstacles in business. This is a month favorable to the female and unfavorable to the male; they will feel an upsurge of emotion, sometimes happy and sometimes sad. They should not act as a guarantor. They should pay attention to problems in blood circulation. Their love life improves just like the sky clears up after the rain and will lead to a happy ending.

Those born in the spring must be on guard against accidents.

8th month (August 29th to September 27th, 2000)
A month with panic and danger

Prospects will rise and fall sharply; there will be the possibility of drowning; fortunately, a lucky star will shine on high; though those born in the year of the rooster may feel shocked, there will be nothing dangerous. It's a sweet month for lovers. But they must be cautious not let a third party spoil their happiness. They must take good care of themselves.

9th month (September 28th to October 26th, 2000)
A month that leans towards stability

Prospects turn out to be good and steady this month; it's suitable to carry out new plans. Sexual life is rich and colorful and an unfulfilled good match might be restored and made, which may cause trouble and quarrels at home. The client had better keep away from alcohol and women.

10th month (October 27th to November 25th, 2000)
A month in which there is much improvement

There is much improvement in prospects this month; more money can be made this month; new opportunities are expected; and it's profitable to invest. But it will not wise to be too impatient for success. Those born in the year of the rooster must be careful not to make mistakes and prevent against thefts and take good care for themselves; they had better not visit the bereaved. Some progress is made

in matters of love and clients may make further progress in this respect.

11th month (November 26th to December 25th, 2000)
A month not to stir up trouble

Fortune is good and business will flourish this month. Clients will enjoy a good reputation and are their glory; they will often travel to a distant land and will be fatigued by a journey; they had better mind their own business and the most important thing is to make their resolutions for the coming year. Those born in spring and summer are not as happy as those born in autumn and winter.

12th month (December 26th, 2000
to January 23rd, 2001)
A month to advance steadily

This is a month to make steady progress; and opportunities to make money will be good; those born in the year of the rooster can make resolutions for the coming year, yet their assessment of risk should be a little bit higher. Their love life is rich and colorful. They had better to snatch a moment from their busy schedule to enjoy the simple joys of life.

DOG

LUCK

There is much improvement in prospects for those born in the year of the dog. If they can seize the opportunity, they might advance rapidly and achieve positions of power. If they are not on good terms with others, those in high positions may be cool towards them.

School children and young students will be successful in their studies this year. But they will be liable to become involved in quarrels and must be guarded in their speech so as not to incur the displease of others.

Housewives who follow their husband's wishes while find that the family in harmony. Yet relatives and friends may spread rumors and lies; they must calmly cope with all kinds of complicated situations. They should never be preoccupied with personal gains and losses. Girls born in the year of the dog should not demand too much on their lovers, for they might break off relations with the boys and feel extremely lonely.

Their luck in making money will be inconsistent this year. Both regular and outside income will fluctuate widely. They must seize the right time when investing of gambling. Those born in the year of the dog must get to know their partners well and they should never judge a person by their appearance. They had better understand the merits of their friend and stand up for them. In this way they will not miss a chance to make a happy match.

Females born in the year of the dog must guard against miscarriage. Children born in 1994 should always be accompanied by an adult when they go out in order to avoid accidents.

Those born in the year of the dog will have good luck in developing and enlarging their undertakings; their reputation will be enhanced, the better to mop up previous bad luck, and they will have bright prospects. They may fall out with brothers and partners and become enemies with each other.

Prospects for those born in the year of the dog tend to be favorable; their fortune and power will increase with each passing day. If they strive for progress and want to achieve good results they may well succeed. They may find noble benefactors help them and can attack or defend as they please; a large number of students will come top of the list in provincial or municipal examinations; civil servants will have the chance of being promoted or taking up advanced studies. They have to take good care of themselves; when reluctant to leave a place with spirits and women, they must warn themselves, so as to avoid suffering unexpected personal financial losses and contracting a disease. If they can consolidate every step, they will be safe and sound. If mean-spirited persons sow discord, they must forgive and dismiss them with a smile. If one is generous, he or she will have good luck. The best matches are with those born in the year of the horse or pig; those born in the year of the dog are under a ban.

ROMANTIC LIFE

In 2000, those born in the year of the dog will be very popular. The best months for them to make love are the 1st and 2nd lunar months. They might hesitate when the arrow of love shoots them, thus missing a good match. During the 5th lunar month another opportunity arrives at their door. Only in winter should they take the initiative in love affairs. The 9th lunar month is the third-best opportunity for them to find the man or woman of their dreams.

They are sincere and honest in love affairs. But they will have trouble and heartache, because their moods fluctuate wildly.

Those born in the year of the dog will get on well with the people born in the year of the horse, tiger and rabbit. It is not suitable for them to marry those born in the year of the ox, dragon, ram or rooster.

Auspicious Colors: green, white.
Inauspicious Colors: red, grey.
Auspicious Numbers: 5 & 9.

FORECASTS BY MONTH
1st month (February 5th to March 5th, 2000)
A lucky and prosperous month

Prospects are both lucky and fortunate; it is a good beginning to the year. Those born in the year are elated at their successes and their dreams may come true. Opportunity in making big money will be very good; their regular and extra income will be sufficient. The elderly might meet with accidents. If they quarrel with their spouse, they may have to restrain themselves. They should keep to a work routine; they must fully abide by the law and do their duty; they must be content with their lot, get ready to fight and accept new challenges.

2nd month (March 6th to April 4th, 2000)
A smooth month

Prospects are good and it will be a suitable time to change a job. Songbirds will choose the best tree to perch on. Meanwhile, those born in the year of the dog will have luck in making money; it will be a suitable time for them to go traveling, seek new opportunities and open up new markets. But they must be on guard against accidents; there are many mean-spirited persons who will set a trap and sow discord, so they must keep alert. Fortunately they will find noble benefactors to support them. They will get through, but they must take good care of themselves.

3rd month (April 5th to May 3rd, 2000)
A month to sharpen vigilance

This is a month to be vigilant, an unlucky one overall. Prospects take a turn for the worse. Things are made difficult for those born in year of the dog; they can be fearless in the face of peril if things are done with confidence; they can never be careless if they want to avoid misfortunes. Family fortunes are not good; friends of spirits and women come in an endless train and they should be kept away from. They must guard against sex traps; they have to resist temptation by members of the opposite sex.

4th month (May 4th to June 1st, 2000)
A month for the fog to clear

Prospects are rather unsteady this month; sometimes good, sometimes bad. Luck in making big money is not so good. Those born in the year of the dog should not invest or gamble. They should keep away from mean-spirited persons and take precautions against marriage breakdown. A beautiful woman may assist them, but they must harbor no evil intentions so as to get a breakthrough in business. Unfortunately luck in making big money will not be good; they should manage to in a manner appropriate with the situation.

5th month (June 2nd to July 1st, 2000)
A month during which all is well

Prospects take a turn for the better this month, but money comes and goes and there will none at hand for emergencies. Noble benefactors will turn up and guide them and they may turn ill luck into good. Their luck in making money begin to turn for the better and all is well; they will gain fame, fortune, and power. This is the best month of the year for those born in the dog year. Beautiful women may press forward; but they shouldn't let their goals be disturbed.

6th month (July 2nd to July 30th, 2000)
A month full of noble aspirations

This is a month imbued with a lofty spirit. Those born in the year of the dog will have good luck in

making money; regular and extra income will be sufficient, yet they must take precautions against possible difficulties and adjust to changing circumstances. They have to guard against opponents of the opposite sex and they should never take things lightly.

7th month (July 31st to August 28th, 2000)
A month for prospects to be inconstant

New conditions bring a challenge and ill luck will be hidden in good luck. Those born in the year of the dog had better take defense as a means of offense. It's suitable for them to travel to a distant land this month. They must guard against danger while living in peace and had better not go in for risky undertakings. Their love life is rich and colorful; it's the right time for those born in 1970 to choose their partner while others born in the year of the dog should have extramarital affairs.

8th month (August 29th to September 27th, 2000)
A month to climb up the peak again

This is a month to be full of noble aspirations and climb up the peak again. Those born in the year of the dog must try to gain the initiative and seek new opportunities; they ought to be cautious not incite quarrels and disputes. Their love life will be rich and colorful, but they must be careful not have extramarital affairs. Near mid-autumn they may suffer calamity and unexpected financial losses or fall ill.

9th month (September 28th to October 26th, 2000)
A month that is rather flat

Prospects will be rather flat this month. After basking in glory, those born in the year of the dog might feel loneliness and tiredness. They must pay attention to interpersonal relationships and take good care of themselves. In dull life they can seek excitement and relax themselves by minor gambling and gain a little extra income, but they must keep away from sex traps.

10th month (October 27th to November 25th, 2000)
A happy month

Prospects take a turn for the better and things will go smoothly. Those born in the year of the dog may give full play to their grand plans yet again; their undertakings will boom, but they had better draw in their horns in matters to do with speculation. They will be nearly invincible since they will find noble benefactors to help them. Females born in the year of the dog must restrain themselves; they must pay attention to safety in daily life and walk less during the night. They ought to attach great importance to diet. The family is in harmony and the wife echoes what the husband sings.

11th month (November 26th to December 25th, 2000)
A month to be cautious when speaking

Prospects will be inconstant this month; sometimes lucky, sometimes unlucky.

Those born in the year of the dog must be cautious

in speech and actions so as not to get in trouble with officials. They must be careful not to injure their head and upper body. Those born in 1958 ought to take good care of the elderly in their family. During the month they'd better not to travel to a distant land or visit the bereaved so as to avoid trouble.

12th month (December 26th, 2000 to January 23rd, 2001)
A month to lay foundations

Prospects will be steady this month; all is well; regular income is sufficient, but it's unwise to long for more. Those who sit for university entrance examinations will be successful. Those who have something to do with the opposite sex should just talk about professional work instead of love, or the gain will be no compensation for the loss. Those born in the year of the dog may find noble benefactors to guide them; they should keep going up steadily and lay a good foundation for the coming year's great plan.

PIG

LUCK

Those born in the year of the pig, especially females, will have good luck throughout the year.

School children and young students born in the year of the pig will make great progress this year if they work hard. But they must pay attention to their health and remember that illness finds its way in by the mouth. Housewives born in the year of the pig will get on well with one another at home. But they must take care of themselves, because their vital energy and circulatory system will be deficient. Their children must be careful not to swallow a foreign body.

Girls born in the year of the pig will yearn for love this year and may meet a lover in the latter half of the year. But they must see clearly to avoid choosing the wrong partner.

As far as luck in making big money is concerned, it may appear to be good but actually it is not. So they must not act rashly. Their luck in making money might turn for better in the latter half of the year.

They are not in very good health this year. They must protect heart and lungs; between autumn and winter they must be careful not to catch cold.

Those born in the year of the pig might have their wishes fulfilled; they have an opportunity to meet that special someone. Love needs cultivating so that it can blossom and bear fruit. Males born in the year of the pig should be very cautious if they have something new to do or start a new job. Females will be lucky if they want to do business or go to work. Even housewives will bring good luck to the family, and their husbands and children are flourishing and prosperous. Married men are liable to fall into traps of a sexual nature which will make great discord with their partners.

They will probably be not be very lucky this year. But they will be able to find noble benefactors to assist them and so achieve progress. As diseases are easily spread they must take good care of them-

selves; meanwhile, they ought to avoid such things as traffic accidents, operations and other disasters. They have to stand up to all tests in love; they must deal with the clashes between husband and wife; never should they fall into sex-trap.

This year diplomatic relationships will be favorable to their development when they are abroad. But they might have a sense of loneliness and must take special care of themselves. They will have opportunities to pursue their goals, but they might experience all sorts of difficulties and hardships. They will have less bad luck and more good luck this year. They might go traveling for pleasure or for business. They will have good luck in doing business and making money; they should act boldly in order to make progress. Those born in the year of the pig may win a good reputation and will gain more skills in areas where they excel. They should do work such as woodwork. And will have plenty of chances to develop themselves. They are quick-witted and versatile; they can become outstanding in public relations and art. They will live a peaceful and pleasant life. Those born in the year of the pig should chose potential mates of those born in the year of the ram and the rabbit.

ROMANTIC LIFE

To those born in the year of the pig, love is not the most important thing in life. But they are very energetic and need the opposite sex to adjust their body and mind. To them, love is an article to exchange. Those born in summer of the year of the pig may reach the peak of love in the 11th and 12th lunar months. During the year love from the opposite sex may bring them stability, cheerfulness and happiness.

Those born in winter may reach the peak of love in the 4th, 5th, 7th, and 8th lunar months. The opposite sex might bring them entanglement, anxiety and agony. These are simply a series of coincidences and new favorable turns in the 7th and 8th month that makes the year of 2000 a colorful one.

Those born in the year of the pig aged 30 to 50 will be more loving to their spouse and show more concern for them than last year. This is because it would be a heavy blow to them if their spouse were to transfer their love to another. Generally speaking, those born in the spring of the pig year are able to handle matters in love calmly. Of the 12 animals, they are the freer and easier and in a sense have a better understanding of human life. Their best matches are with those born in the year of the ram, tiger or rabbit. They ought to avoid marrying those born in the year of the snake, monkey or pig.

Auspicious Colors: black, yellow.
Inauspicious Colors: red, green.
Auspicious Numbers: 4 & 7.

FORECASTS BY MONTH
1st month (February 5th to March 5th, 2000)
A month to observe quietly

Prospects will be unsteady and unpredictable. It will be hard to seek fame and fortune. There will not be much luck in making money. There will be turns and zigzags in their professional work. Those born in the year of the dog and had better observe situations quietly and take good care of their health. They must take precautions against accidents, in particular their limbs. Females are luckier than males this month.

2nd month (March 6th to April 4th, 2000)
A month favorable to the female

Fate trends tend to be very smooth this month. But those born in the pig year shouldn't make premature advance in work. Wherever they go, they may find noble benefactors to assist them and problems can be readily solved. This month is more favorable to the female. They had better not visit the bereaved, thus avoiding misfortunes and tending towards prosperity.

3rd month (April 5th to May 3rd, 2000)
A month of surprise and joy

This month is a lucky one. Those born in the year of the pig will have been looking forward to it, a month of mixed feelings, of surprise and joy. Financial resources will be sufficient and their fame will rise with each passing day. Those born in winter might gain more. Females born in the year of the pig will have good luck in making money. The married should guard against sex traps; they should never ruin their professional work because of personal relationships.

4th month (May 4th to June 1st, 2000)
A month that turns for the worse

This is an unlucky month, during which prospects take a turn for the worse. Undertakings will not go smoothly; one quarrel will follow another; luck in making money is not so good; there will be twists and turns. Those born in the year of the pig must cope with adversity calmly. With the help of noble benefactors they will surely get through. They must avoid getting involved in love affairs and must respond to the changing situation without panicking. It is not suitable for them to go on a long journey.

5th month (June 2nd to July 1st, 2000)
A month rising from bottom to top

This month will be prosperous. They will start at the bottom and make giant strides toward the top. Those born in the year of the big will make great

progress in their undertakings; there will be good luck in making money. Those born in the year of the pig must calmly deal with money matters, disputes between friends and involvement in love affairs. After they get rid of such troublesome things they can bring order out of chaos.

6th month (July 2nd to July 30th, 2000)
A month for good luck to continue

Prospects remain good. Those born in the year of the pig might be daring enough to reverse the course of events; they will meet with one happy event after another; regular and extra income will be sufficient to meet their needs. The important thing is harmony in dealing with interpersonal relationships, which will enable them to be long lasting. Noble benefactors will be found to guide them; they can gain by visiting famous rivers and mountains; their love life will be rich and colorful; when happy events occur, they will be full of enthusiasm and lead a happy family life.

7th month (July 31st to August 28th, 2000)
A month when fortune smiles

Those born in the year of the pig can gain fame, wealth, and power. They must remember that good luck and bad luck often go together. They ought to avoid speculation and should be able to distinguish between right and wrong.

8th month (August 29th to September 27th, 2000)
A month of surprises

This is a month for new prospects to show up suddenly. But those born in the year of the pig must be cautious not to get lost and not to mislead themselves. Noble benefactors will be of the opposite sex; to ensure family safety, they must not fall in love with each other. It is right time for them to purchase houses or land. Those born in the spring and summer must sharpen their vigilance in order to get a clear understanding of the situation.

9th month (September 28th to October 26th, 2000)
A month to take retreat as a means to advance

Prospects will be rather overcast and gloomy; success in business is not on the horizon. Those born in the year of the pig had better not invest, but they will still be able to broaden their horizons. They must be careful to deal with money matters and pay attention to safety of the family. Their love life will be on an even keel, but they should not harbor any audacious ambition; they will find favor in the eyes of the opposite sex, but they must keep them at a distance so as not to get entangled.

10th month (October 27th to November 25th, 2000)
A month where work will be rewarded

There's slight improvement in fortune this month. Anxiety will disappear gradually. Those born in the year of the pig must seize the opportunity if the time is right, but they should not be too impatient for success. During the month they may get more

pay for more work; they will not only have a regular income but also extra income. They will still be down on their luck; they had better not visit the bereaved; they should not place too much trust in friendship so as not to suffer unexpected financial losses. They are elated by their love life and are envied by others. Those born in summer are the earliest to get rid of embarrassment; those born in spring are the most capable in coping with the current conditions.

11th month (November 26th to December 25th, 2000)
A month to gain both love and wealth

This month is luckier than last month; there will be sufficient luck in making money; friendships will be satisfactory; it's the right time for those who remain single to choose a spouse. They must be on guard against traffic accidents and intestinal and stomach diseases.

12th month (December 26th, 2000
to January 23rd, 2001)
A month of many happy events

This is a lucky month. Luck in making money will be very good; a high reputation will be enjoyed. The middle-aged born in the year of the pig will gain both fame and wealth. Young people born in the year of the pig will make great progress in their studies. It is a suitable time for them to travel to a distant land and earn a living, but they must keep away from situations where they have to decide between right and wrong. Their love life is rich and

colorful, but they must be cautious not to fall into sexual traps. They must get ready to greet the coming year with brilliant achievements.

Months of the Dragon Year

Lunar month	Solar date
1st	5 February to 5 March 2000
2nd	6 March to 4 April 2000
3rd	5 April to 3 May 2000
4th	4 May to 1 June 2000
5th	2 June to 1 July 2000
6th	2 July to 30 July 2000
7th	31 July to 28 August 2000
8th	29 August to 27 September 2000
9th	28 September to 26 October 2000
10th	27 October to 25 November 2000
11th	26 November to 25 December 2000
12th	26 December 2000 to 23 January 2001

Dates of Lunar Years

18.02.1912 to 05.02.1913: RAT
06.02.1913 to 25.01.1914: OX
26.01.1914 to 13.02.1915: TIGER
14.02.1915 to 02.02.1916: RABBIT
03.02.1916 to 22.01.1917: DRAGON
23.01.1917 to 10.02.1918: SNAKE
11.02.1918 to 31.01.1919: HORSE
01.02.1919 to 19.02.1920: RAM
20.02.1920 to 07.02.1921: MONKEY
08.02.1921 to 27.01.1922: ROOSTER
28.01.1922 to 15.02.1923: DOG
16.02.1923 to 04.02.1924: PIG

05.02.1924 to 24.01.1925: RAT
25.01.1925 to 12.02.1926: OX
13.02.1926 to 01.02 1927: TIGER
02.02.1927 to 22.01.1928: RABBIT
23.01.1928 to 09.02.1929: DRAGON
10.02.1929 to 29.01.1930: SNAKE
30.01.1930 to 16.02.1931: HORSE
17.02.1931 to 05.02.1932: RAM
06.02.1932 to 25.01.1933: MONKEY
26.01.1933 to 13.02.1934: ROOSTER
14.02.1934 to 03.02.1935: DOG
04.02.1935 to 23.01.1936: PIG

24.01.1936 to 10.02.1937: RAT
11.02.1937 to 30.01.1938: OX
31.01.1938 to 18.02.1939: TIGER
19.02.1939 to 07.02.1940: RABBIT
08.02.1940 to 26.01.1941: DRAGON
27.01.1941 to 14.02.1942: SNAKE
15.02.1942 to 04.02.1943: HORSE
05.02.1943 to 24.01.1944: RAM
25.01.1944 to 12.02.1945: MONKEY
13.02.1945 to 01.02.1946: ROOSTER
02.02.1946 to 21.01.1947: DOG
22.01.1947 to 09.02.1948: PIG

10.02.1948 to 28.01.1949: RAT
29.01.1949 to 16.02.1950: OX
17.02.1950 to 05.02.1951: TIGER
06.02.1951 to 26.01.1952: RABBIT
27.01.1952 to 13.02.1953: DRAGON
14.02.1953 to 02.02.1954: SNAKE
03.02.1954 to 23.01.1955: HORSE
24.01.1955 to 11.02.1956: RAM
12.02.1956 to 30.01 1957: MONKEY
31.01.1957 to 17.02.1958: ROOSTER
18.02.1958 to 07.02.1959: DOG
08.02.1959 to 27.01.1960: PIG

28.01.1960 to 14.02.1961: RAT
15.02.1961 to 04.02.1962: OX
05.02.1962 to 24.01.1963: TIGER
25.01.1963 to 12.02.1964: RABBIT
13.02.1964 to 01.02.1965: DRAGON
02.02.1965 to 20.01.1966: SNAKE
21.01.1966 to 08.02.1967: HORSE
09.02.1967 to 29.01.1968: RAM
30.01.1968 to 16.02.1969: MONKEY
17.02.1969 to 05.02.1970: ROOSTER
06.02.1970 to 26.01.1971: DOG
27.01.1971 to 14.02.1972: PIG

15.02.1972 to 02.02.1973: RAT
03.02.1973 to 22.01.1974: OX
23.01.1974 to 10.02.1975: TIGER
11.02.1975 to 30.01.1976: RABBIT
31.01.1976 to 17.02.1977: DRAGON
18.02.1977 to 06.02.1978: SNAKE
07.02.1978 to 27.01.1979: HORSE
28.01.1979 to 15.02.1980: RAM
16.02.1980 to 04.02.1981: MONKEY
05.02.1981 to 24.01.1982: ROOSTER
25.01.1982 to 12.02.1983: DOG
13.02.1983 to 01.02.1984: PIG

02.02.1984 to 19.02.1985: RAT
20.02.1985 to 08.02.1986: OX
09.02.1986 to 28.01.1987: TIGER
29.01.1987 to 16.02.1988: RABBIT
17.02.1988 to 05.02.1989: DRAGON
06.02.1989 to 26.01.1990: SNAKE
27.01.1990 to 14.02.1991: HORSE
15.02.1991 to 03.02.1992: RAM
04.02.1992 to 22.01.1993: MONKEY
23.01.1993 to 09.02.1994: ROOSTER
10.02.1994 to 30.01.1995: DOG
31.01.1995 to 18.02.1996: PIG

19.02.1996 to 06.02.1997: RAT
07.02.1997 to 27.01.1998: OX
28.01.1998 to 15.02.1999: TIGER
16.02.1999 to 04.02.2000: RABBIT
05.02.2000 to 23.01.2001: DRAGON
24.01.2001 to 11.02.2002: SNAKE
12.02.2002 to 31.01.2003: HORSE
01.02.2003 to 21.01.2004: RAM
22.01.2004 to 08.02.2005: MONKEY
09.02.2005 to 28.01.2006: ROOSTER
29.01.2006 to 17.02.2007: DOG
18.02.2007 to 06.02.2008: PIG

Predicting the Sex of a Child

12	11	10	9	8	7	6	5	4	3	2	1	Lunar month of conception / Mother's age
M	M	M	M	M	M	M	M	M	F	M	F	18
F	F	M	M	M	M	M	F	F	M	F	M	19
M	M	F	M	M	M	M	M	M	F	M	F	20
F	F	F	F	F	F	F	F	F	F	F	M	21
F	F	F	F	M	F	F	M	F	M	M	F	22
F	M	M	M	F	M	F	M	M	F	M	M	23
F	F	F	F	F	M	M	F	M	M	F	M	24
M	M	M	M	M	F	M	F	F	M	M	F	25
F	F	F	F	M	F	M	F	F	M	F	M	26
M	F	M	M	M	M	F	F	M	F	M	F	27
F	M	M	M	M	M	F	F	F	M	M	M	28
F	F	F	M	M	M	M	M	F	F	M	F	29
M	M	F	F	F	F	F	F	F	F	F	M	30
M	F	F	F	F	F	F	F	F	M	F	M	31
M	F	F	F	F	F	F	F	F	M	F	M	32
M	F	F	F	M	F	F	F	M	F	M	F	33
M	M	F	F	F	F	F	F	F	M	F	M	34
M	M	F	F	M	F	F	F	M	F	M	M	35
M	M	M	M	F	F	F	M	F	M	M	F	36
M	F	M	F	M	F	M	F	M	F	M	M	37
F	M	F		F	M	F	M	M	F	M	F	38
F	F	M	F	M	F	F	M	M	M	F	M	39
F	M	F	M	F	M	M	F	M	F	M	F	40
M	F	M	F	M	M	F	M	F	M	F	M	41
F	F	M	M	M	F	M	F	M	F	M	F	42
M	M	M	M	F	M	F	M	F	M	F	M	43
F	F	M	F	M	F	M	M	M	F	M	M	44
M	M	F	M	F	M	F	F	F	M	M	F	45

JANUARY 2000 / *12th month of the Rabbit year*

Day	Date			Activities
Sa	1	25	●	☆ unlucky day: no activities ✖ open stores; buy houses or land
Su	2	26	○	☆ building work; move house; hunt; hairstyling ✖ pray for fertility; stock speculation; fishing
Mo	3	27	●	☆ visit; make offerings to gods; study; adoption ✖ lay foundations; prepare wedding bed
Tu	4	28	●	☆ unlucky day: no activities ✖ make wine; visit friends; lay foundations
We	5	29	○	☆ make offerings to gods; engagements; house building ✖ adopt a child; hunt; fish; paint walls
Th	6	30	○	☆ kitchen work; install furnaces ❑ Slight Cold ✖ do odd jobs; buy houses; legal trial; marriage
Fr	7	XII	○	☆ new clothes; travel; open stores; swim ✖ building work; lay foundations; buy houses
Sa	8	2	○	☆ make offerings to gods; engagements; visit friends; adoption ✖ garden work; lay foundations
Su	9	3	○	☆ swim; housecleaning; marriage; move house ✖ travel; offerings to gods; kitchen work
Mo	10	4	○	☆ offerings to ancestors; garden work; travel; engagements ✖ pray for fertility; dig wells; hairstyling
Tu	11	5	○	☆ offerings to ancestors; marriage; travel ✖ move house; buy houses or land
We	12	6	●	☆ visit; sign contracts; marriage; new clothes ✖ travel; mourning
Th	13	7	●	☆ make offerings to ancestors; travel; lay foundations; visit ✖ repair fishing nets; bathroom work
Fr	14	8	●	☆ unlucky day: no activities ✖ make wine; make preserves
Sa	15	9	○	☆ offerings to ancestors; move house; hairstyling ✖ prepare wedding bed; irrigation work
Su	16	10	●	☆ unlucky day: no activities ✖ sow crops; dig wells; legal trial
Mo	17	11	○	☆ offerings to ancestors; hunt; install furnaces ✖ launch business; do business
Tu	18	12	●	☆ offerings to gods; study; visit; adoption ✖ fish; marriage; sow crops; mourning
We	19	13	○	☆ offerings to ancestors; funerals; new clothes ✖ launch business; acupuncture; kitchen work
Th	20	14	○	☆ move house; sign contracts ✖ funerals; deliver goods; hairstyling; kitchen work
Fr	21	15	●	☆ lunar eclipse: unlucky day ❑ Great Cold ✖ buy houses; make offerings to ancestors; lay foundations
Sa	22	16	○	☆ offerings to ancestors; engagements; give dowries ✖ visit the sick; dig wells or ponds
Su	23	17	○	☆ offerings to gods; garden work; marriage; give dowry ✖ repair fishing nets
Mo	24	18	●	☆ offerings to ancestors; visit friends; engagements; ✖ sow crops; travel; make wine
Tu	25	19	○	☆ hairstyling; manicure babies; travel; funerals ✖ visit the sick; irrigation work
We	26	20	●	☆ unlucky day: no activities ✖ do business; legal trial
Th	27	21	●	☆ make offerings; travel; study; hairstyling; funerals ✖ prepare wedding bed; deliver goods
Fr	28	22	●	☆ unlucky day: no activities ✖ visit; fish; hunt; sow crops
Sa	29	23	○	☆ make offerings to gods; fish; hunt; travel ✖ kitchen work; do business
Su	30	24	○	☆ offerings to gods; study; housecleaning ✖ marriage; sign contracts; hairstyling
Mo	31	25	○	☆ make offerings to ancestors; swim; travel; do business ✖ garden work; buy houses or land

● lucky day   ○ neutral day   ● unlucky day   ❑ 24 solar terms
☆ auspicious activity   ✖ inauspicious activity

FEBRUARY 2000 / *1st month of the Dragon year*

Tu	1	26	○	☆ make offerings to ancestors; engagements; paint walls ✖ funerals; lay foundations
We	2	27	○	☆ travels; marriage; hairstyling; immigration; funerals ✖ make offerings to ancestors; launch business
Th	3	28	●	☆ unlucky day: no activity ✖ make wine; dig wells
Fr	4	29	●	☆ hunt; fish; ❐ Beginning of Spring ✖ dig wells; hydraulic work
Sa	5	lst	●	☆ Year of the Dragon begins, God of Fortune in the South ✖ trials; gardening
Su	6	2	●	☆ offerings; visits to friends; marriage; build houses ✖ inside work; funerals
Mo	7	3	○	☆ hunt; fish; train; build houses ✖ sow crops; gardening
Tu	8	4	●	☆ unlucky day: no activity ✖ commercial activities; kitchen work
We	9	5	○	☆ offerings; travel; marriage; new clothes; funerals ✖ visits; hairstyling; hunt; fish
Th	10	6	●	☆ unlucky day: no activity ✖ marriage; move house; buy house
Fr	11	7	●	☆ visits; adoptions; baths; acupuncture; hairstyling ✖ marriage; funerals; lay foundations
Sa	12	8	○	☆ make offerings; study; travel; marriage ✖ fishing net repair; lay foundations
Su	13	9	○	☆ make offerings to ancestors; paint walls ✖ make wine; acupuncture
Mo	14	10	●	☆ engagements; new clothes; funerals; visit friends ✖ offerings to ancestors; build dams
Tu	15	11	○	☆ travels; baths; hairstyling; contracts; funerals ✖ dig wells or ponds; legal trials
We	16	12	○	☆ offerings to ancestors; visit friends; new clothes ✖ funerals; deliver goods
Th	17	13	○	☆ garden work; interior decoration ✖ travel; sow crops; prepare the marriage bed
Fr	18	14	●	☆ make offerings; study; travel; marriage; funerals ✖ kitchen work; bathroom work; furnace installation
Sa	19	15	○	☆ make offerings; open a shop ❐ Rain Water ✖ hairstyling; fish
Su	20	16	●	☆ unlucky day: no activity ✖ buy houses or land; prepare the marriage bed
Mo	21	17	○	☆ make offerings; hairstyling; build houses; funerals ✖ sow crops; commercial activities; boat christening
Tu	22	18	●	☆ unlucky day: no activity ✖ marriage; funerals; repair fishing nets
We	23	19	○	☆ build houses; travel; immigration ✖ marriage; make wine; make preserves
Th	24	20	●	☆ study; visits; new clothes; marriage ✖ repair gutters; drain water
Fr	25	21	○	☆ prepare weddings; kitchen work; paint walls ✖ legal trials; lay foundations
Sa	26	22	○	☆ visit friends; new clothes; adoptions ✖ make offerings; make deliveries; selling
Su	27	23	●	☆ marriage; hairstyling; study; lay foundations ✖ dig wells; sow crops
Mo	28	24	○	☆ make offerings; lay foundations; marriage, funerals ✖ kitchen work; install furnaces
Tu	29	25	○	☆ make footpaths; paint walls ✖ travel; hairstyling

● lucky day ○ neutral day ● unlucky day ❐ 24 solar terms
☆ auspicious activity ✖ inauspicious activity

MARCH 2000 / *2nd month of the Dragon year*

We	1	26	●	☆ make offerings; visits; marriage; open stores ✖ buy houses; bathroom work
Th	2	27	○	☆ make offerings; study; visits; funerals ✖ kitchen work; attic repairs
Fr	3	28	●	☆ unlucky day; no activity ✖ repair fishing nets; prepare weddings
Sa	4	29	○	☆ make offerings; sign contracts; business; funerals ✖ make wine; make preserves
Su	5	30	●	☆ unlucky days; ❏ Awakening from hibernation ✖ travel; build irrigation; christen boats
Mo	6	11	○	☆ study; launch business; new clothes ✖ marriage; engagements; mourning clothes
Tu	7	2	○	☆ make offerings to ancestors; hunt; hairstyling; sow crops ✖ deliver goods; receive money
We	8	3	●	☆ study; new clothes; marriage; adoption ✖ sow crops; build walls; funerals
Th	9	4	○	☆ study; visit friends; adoption ✖ kitchen work; install furnaces; make offerings to ancestors
Fr	10	5	○	☆ visits; travel; marriage; construction work, move house ✖ hairstyling; interior decoration; dig wells
Sa	11	6	○	☆ travels; hairstyling; manicure babies; paint walls ✖ make offerings to gods; engagements; funerals
Su	12	7	○	☆ engagements; marriage; send dowries; open a store ✖ travel; move house; lay foundations
Mo	13	8	○	☆ repair paths; paint walls ✖ repair fishing nets; bathroom work
Tu	14	9	●	☆ visit friends; offerings; marriage; build houses ✖ acupuncture; make wine
We	15	10	○	☆ swim; hairstyling; clean; end mourning; funerals ✖ gutter work; prepare the marriage bed
Th	16	11	●	☆ unlucky day; no activity ✖ move house; launch business; trials
Fr	17	12	●	☆ unlucky day; no activities ✖ make deliveries; receive money
Sa	18	13	●	☆ hairstyling; visit doctors; study; adoptions ✖ marriage; sow crops; end mourning
Su	19	14	●	☆ unlucky day: no activity ✖ marriage; kitchen work
Mo	20	15	●	☆ travel; adoptions ❏ Spring Equinox ✖ hairstyling; funerals
Tu	21	16	○	☆ construction work; kitchen work; paint walls; funerals ✖ make offerings to gods; acupuncture; buy houses
We	22	17	○	☆ travel; visit friends; clean; swim ✖ visit patients; funerals; dig wells
Th	23	18	●	☆ go out; swim; hairstyling; manicure babies; clean ✖ repair fishing nets; funerals
Fr	24	19	○	☆ pray for happiness; visit friends; sign contracts ✖ make wine; lay foundations
Sa	25	20	○	☆ make offerings to gods; repair paths; paint walls ✖ gutter work; bathroom work
Su	26	21	●	☆ marriage; visit friends; sign contracts; funerals ✖ trials; christen boats; acupuncture
Mo	27	22	○	☆ study; marriage; hairstyling; funerals ✖ deliveries; preparation of the marriage bed
Tu	28	23	●	☆ unlucky day: no activity ✖ christen boats
We	29	24	●	☆ unlucky day: no activity ✖ kitchen work; install furnaces
Th	30	25	●	☆ make offerings; travel; study; construction work ✖ hairstyling; marriage; end mourning
Fr	31	26	○	☆ marriage; engagements; hairstyling; hunt; fish ✖ buy houses or property

APRIL 2000 / 3th month of the Dragon year

Sa	1	27	●	☆ make offerings; study; travel; marriage; hairstyling ✖ cut of trees; paint walls; funerals
Su	2	28	○	☆ build houses; sign contracts; funerals ✖ repair fishing nets; make offerings to ancestors
Mo	3	29	○	☆ travels; visit friends; contracts; business ✖ lay foundations; dig wells
Tu	4	30	○	☆ travels; swim; hairstyling; clean ⬚ Pure Brightness ✖ irrigation works; drain water
We	5	III	●	☆ clean; build houses; cut trees ✖ trials; travel
Th	6	2	○	☆ make offerings; new clothes; repair fishing nets; funerals ✖ deliveries; bathroom works
Fr	7	3	○	☆ make offerings; fish; repair paths; paint walls ✖ christen boats
Sa	8	4	○	☆ construction work; clean; new clothes; funerals ✖ prepare marriage beds; kitchen work
Su	9	5	○	☆ make offerings; marriage; send dowries; contracts ✖ hairstyling; lay foundations
Mo	10	6	●	☆ unlucky day: no activities ✖ make offerings to ancestors; prepare weddings
Tu	11	7	●	☆ demolitions; swim ✖ buy houses; funerals
We	12	8	○	☆ study; visit; travel; build houses ✖ trials; repair fishing nets
Th	13	9	○	☆ make offerings; build houses; adoptions ✖ make wine; make preserves
Fr	14	10	○	☆ study; visit; marriage; new clothes ✖ make offerings to ancestors; acupuncture; drain water
Sa	15	11	○	☆ kitchen work; paint walls; funerals ✖ launch business; legal trials; dig wells
Su	16	12	○	☆ make offerings; paint walls; hairstyling ✖ marriage; engagements; deliveries; lay foundations
Mo	17	13	●	☆ swim; hairstyling; clean; construction work ✖ travel; sow crops
Tu	18	14	○	☆ make offerings; marriage; mourning; funerals ✖ kitchen work; install furnaces
We	19	15	○	☆ paint walls; reapair paths ✖ hairstyling; manicure babies
Th	20	16	○	☆ make offerings; hairstyling; sign contracts ⬚ Grain Rain ✖ buy houses; prepare marriage beds
Fr	21	17	●	☆ visit doctors; marriage; construction work; hairstyling ✖ mourning; lay foundations
Sa	22	18	●	☆ unlucky day: no activities ✖ repair fishing nets; open a store
Su	23	19	○	☆ visit friends; adoptions; receive money ✖ make wine; marriage
Mo	24	20	○	☆ study; visit; hairstyling; adoptions; funeral ✖ irrigation work; drain water
Tu	25	21	○	☆ hunt; install furnaces; adoptions ✖ deliveries; trials
We	26	22	●	☆ study; travel; open a store; visit ✖ make offerings; acupuncture; business
Th	27	23	○	☆ make offerings; travel; lay foundations; funeral ✖ sow crops; dig wells or ponds
Fr	28	24	○	☆ make offerings to ancestors; kitchen works; paint walls ✖ lay foundations; install furnaces
Sa	29	25	○	☆ make offerings; interior decoration; visit; marriage ✖ travel; hairstyling; hunt; end mourning
Su	30	26	○	☆ travels; visit friends; hairstyling; prepare marriage beds ✖ buy houses, land or property

● lucky day ○ neutral day ● unlucky day ⬚ 24 solar terms
☆ auspicious activity ✖ inauspicious activity

MAY 2000 / 4th month of the Dragon year

Mo	1	27	○	☆ hairstyling; hunt; repair paths; paint walls ✖ prepare medicines; medical check
Tu	2	28	●	☆ hairstyling; housecleaning; adopt pets; funerals ✖ repair fishing nets; prepare wedding bed
We	3	29	○	☆ make offerings; hairstyling; medical check; funerals ✖ lay foundations; make wine
Th	4	IV	●	☆ unlucky day: no important activities ✖ irrigation work; drain water
Fr	5	2	●	☆ unlucky day: no activities ❒ Beginning of Summer ✖ legal trial; marriage; engagements;
Sa	6	3	○	☆ visit; building work; marriage; new clothes; funerals ✖ deliver goods; visit fortuneteller; receive payment
Su	7	4	●	☆ make offerings; marriage; give dowries; medical check ✖ sow crops; repair stove; kitchen work
Mo	8	5	○	☆ visit; travel; marriage; give dowries; adoption ✖ make offerings to ancestors; lay foundations; kitchen work
Tu	9	6	○	☆ study; travel; engagements; sow crops ✖ hairstyling; dig wells or ponds
We	10	7	○	☆ paint walls; sign contracts; do business ✖ buy houses; move house; marriage
Th	11	8	○	☆ swim; launch business; repair fishing nets ✖ travel; lay foundations
Fr	12	9	○	☆ visit; travel; marriage; move house ✖ repair fishing nets; bathroom work
Sa	13	10	○	☆ buy houses; interior decoration ✖ make wine; funerals
Su	14	11	○	☆ swim; clean house; paint walls; interior decoration ✖ prepare wedding bed; irrigation work
Mo	15	12	●	☆ travel; study; marriage; house building ✖ sow crops; legal trial; christen a boat
Tu	16	13	●	☆ unlucky day: no activities ✖ install furnaces; deliver goods
We	17	14	●	☆ unlucky day: no activities ✖ garden work; marriage
Th	18	15	●	☆ make offerings; visit; travel; move house ✖ kitchen work; repair stove; end mourning
Fr	19	16	○	☆ study; visit; travel; engagements ✖ hairstyling; manicure babies; legal trial
Sa	20	17	○	☆ house building; hunt; fish; travel ✖ make offerings to ancestors; lay foundations
Su	21	18	●	☆ travel; hairstyling; marriage ❒ Grain Full ✖ dig wells or ponds; lay foundations
Mo	22	19	○	☆ travel; move house; do business ✖ acupuncture; repair fishing nets
Tu	23	20	○	☆ visit; marriage; give dowries; house raising ✖ make wine; travel
We	24	21	○	☆ make offerings; visit; medical check; funerals ✖ dig canals; bathroom work
Th	25	22	○	☆ sow crops; fishing; buy land; paint walls ✖ legal trial; funerals
Fr	26	23	○	☆ marriage; give dowries; housecleaning; repair paths ✖ sell stock; deliver goods
Sa	27	24	●	☆ study; travel; marriage; funerals ✖ sow crops; visit; fish; hunt
Su	28	25	●	☆ unlucky day: no important activities ✖ kitchen work; install furnaces
Mo	29	26	●	☆ unlucky day: no important activities ✖ hairstyling; marriage; cut tree; hunt
Tu	30	27	○	☆ visit; new clothes; marriage; funerals ✖ buy houses; open store
We	31	28	○	☆ study; travel; engagements; new clothes ✖ make offerings to ancestors; legal trial; move house

● lucky day   ○ neutral day   ● unlucky day   ❒ 24 solar terms
☆ auspicious activity   ✖ inauspicious activity

151

JUNE 2000 / 5th month of the Dragon year

				Activities
Th	1	29	○	☆ visit; marriage; move house; funerals ✘ make offerings to ancestors; building work; repair granary
Fr	2	V	●	☆ study; visit; travel; marriage; building work ✘ dig wells; cut trees; make wine
Sa	3	2	○	☆ fish; hunt; marriage; open stores ✘ prepare wedding bed; build dikes
Su	4	3	○	☆ visit; new clothes; change jobs ✘ lay foundations; legal trial; funerals
Mo	5	4	●	☆ marriage; building work; funerals ❏ Grain in Ear ✘ house building; install home appliances
Tu	6	5	●	☆ make offerings to ancestors; marriage; funerals ✘ sow crops; end mourning
We	7	6	○	☆ visit friends; travel; new clothes; funerals ✘ prepare wedding bed; kitchen work
Th	8	7	○	☆ swim; housecleaning; paint walls; repair paths ✘ hairstyling; travel; lay foundations
Fr	9	8	●	☆ unlucky day: no activities ✘ buy land or houses
Sa	10	9	○	☆ make offerings to gods; swim; housecleaning ✘ engagements; marriage; end mourning
Su	11	10	●	☆ unlucky day: no activities ✘ fish; kitchen work; move house
Mo	12	11	○	☆ visit friends; marriage; hairstyling; give dowries ✘ hunt; fish; make wine; christen boat
Tu	13	12	○	☆ study; medical check; house building ✘ move house; irrigation; making offerings
We	14	13	○	☆ make offerings to gods; repair fishing nets; funerals ✘ marriage; engagements; dig wells; legal trial
Th	15	14	○	☆ study; new clothes; travel; engagements; ✘ lay foundations; do business
Fr	16	15	●	☆ unlucky day: no activities ✘ marriage; engagements; sow crops; travel
Sa	17	16	○	☆ lay foundations; funerals; change jobs ✘ kitchen work; house building
Su	18	17	○	☆ visit; travel; marriage; give dowries; adoption ✘ hairstyling; end mourning; new clothes
Mo	19	18	●	☆ make offerings to gods; hairstyling; medical check; housecleaning ✘ buy land; prepare wedding bed
Tu	20	19	●	☆ unlucky day: no activities ✘ kitchen work; travel; funerals
We	21	20	●	☆ unlucky day: no activities ❏ Summer Solstice ✘ sow crops; repair fishing nets
Th	22	21	●	☆ make offerings; visit friends; hairstyling; house building ✘ install home appliances; marriage; make wine
Fr	23	22	●	☆ unlucky day: no activities ✘ marriage; dig canals
Sa	24	23	○	☆ prepare wedding bed; paint walls ✘ lay foundations; legal trial; end mourning
Su	25	24	○	☆ study; hairstyling; engagements; funerals ✘ deliver goods; receive payment
Mo	26	25	○	☆ make offerings to ancestors; fish ✘ sow crops; dig wells
Tu	27	26	○	☆ study; visit; travel; new clothes ✘ kitchen work; cut trees
We	28	27	○	☆ move house; house building ✘ hairstyling; travel; marriage; funerals
Th	29	28	○	☆ make offerings to gods; funerals; paint walls ✘ buy houses; irrigation
Fr	30	29	○	☆ visit; travel; hairstyling; sign contracts ✘ marriage; engagements; medical check

● lucky day   ○ neutral day   ● unlucky day   ❏ 24 solar terms
☆ auspicious activity   ✘ inauspicious activity

JULY 2000 / 6th month of the Dragon year

Sa	1	30	○	☆ make offerings to gods; travel; hairstyling; funerals ✖ lay foundations; install home appliances
Su	2	VI	○	☆ make offerings to gods; hairstyling; swim; manicure babies ✖ travel; make wine; deliver goods
Mo	3	2	●	☆ unlucky day: no activities ✖ irrigation; lay foundations
Tu	4	3	○	☆ make offerings to ancestors; swim; hunt; marriage ✖ legal trial; funerals; end mourning
We	5	4	●	☆ unlucky day: no activities ✖ deliver goods;
Th	6	5	○	☆ make offerings to gods; hairstyling; irrigation; funerals ✖ sow crops; build dikes; pray for fertility
Fr	7	6	○	☆ visit friends; marriage; sow crops ❏ Slight Heat ✖ kitchen work; make offerings to gods
Sa	8	7	○	☆ visit friends; marriage; adoption; do business ✖ hairstyling; legal trial; dig ponds
Su	9	8	○	☆ make offerings to gods; hunt ✖ buy houses, land or property; sharpen knives
Mo	10	9	●	☆ offerings to ancestors; study; hairstyling; do business ✖ travel; end mourning; sharpen knives
Tu	11	10	○	☆ make wine; funerals; do not visit the sick ✖ repair fishing nets; acupuncture; sow crops
We	12	11	○	☆ visit; travel; marriage *1st Dog Days period* ✖ make wine; make preserves
Th	13	12	●	☆ make offerings to ancestors; swim; hairstyling; funerals ✖ irrigation; prepare wedding bed
Fr	14	13	○	☆ make offerings to ancestors; marriage; new clothes ✖ legal trial; acupuncture; hairstyling; funerals
Sa	15	14	●	☆ unlucky day: no important activities ✖ deliver goods; marriage
Su	16	15	○	☆ lunar eclipse: no important activities ✖ sow crops; marriage; buy property; lay foundations
Mo	17	16	●	☆ hairstyling; bathing; manicure babies; hunt; fish ✖ kitchen work; repair stove; visit friends
Tu	18	17	●	☆ unlucky day: no important activities ✖ funerals; building work; open stores
We	19	18	○	☆ travel; engagements; move house; make wine ✖ buy land or property; make offerings to ancestors
Th	20	19	○	☆ study; travel; marriage; adopt pets ✖ dig wells or ponds; begin or end mourning
Fr	21	20	○	☆ hunt; sow crops; garden work *2nd Dog Days period* ✖ repair fishing nets; repair granary
Sa	22	21	○	☆ study; hairstyling ❏ Great Heat ✖ travel; make wine; install home appliances
Su	23	22	○	☆ end mourning; lay foundations; funerals; make wine ✖ irrigation; kitchen work; acupuncture
Mo	24	23	○	☆ visit friends; travel; marriage; open stores ✖ legal trial, lay foundations; engagements; irrigation
Tu	25	24	○	☆ swim; engagements; move house; adopt pets ✖ hunt; prepare wedding bed; travel
We	26	25	○	☆ swim; housecleaning; new clothes; funerals; building work ✖ sow crops; acupuncture; travel; marriage
Th	27	26	●	☆ unlucky day: no activities ✖ kitchen work; demolition; pray for fertility
Fr	28	27	○	☆ visit friends; travel; new clothes; adoption ✖ hairstyling; marriage; begin or finish mourning
Sa	29	28	○	☆ offerings; travel; hairstyling; bath; hunt; new clothes ✖ buy land or, houses; visit fortune teller
Su	30	VII	●	☆ unlucky day: no important activities ✖ begin or finish mourning; funerals; dig wells
Mo	31	2	○	☆ visit friends; open store; give dowries ✖ make offerings to gods; repair fishing nets

● lucky day   ○ neutral day   ● unlucky day   ❏ 24 solar terms
☆ auspicious activity   ✖ inauspicious activity

AUGUST 2000 / 7th month of the Dragon year

Tu	1	2	●	☆ make offerings to gods; study; marriage; visit ✘ make wine; make preserves; dig wells
We	2	3	○	☆ travel; hunt; plantation; receive payment ✘ irrigation; drain water;
Th	3	4	○	☆ study; engagements; new clothes; hairstyling ✘ legal trial; long travel; open stores
Fr	4	5	○	☆ new clothes; paint walls; make wine ✘ deliver goods; bathroom work
Sa	5	6	○	☆ travel; marriage; open stores; house raising ✘ lay foundations; funerals; interior decoration
Su	6	7	●	☆ unlucky day: no activities ✘ kitchen work; prepare wedding bed
Mo	7	8	○	☆ swim; housecleaning ❑ Beginning of Autumn ✘ hairstyling; acupuncture; sow crops; travel
Tu	8	9	○	☆ unlucky day: no activities ✘ buy property or land; fish; house raising
We	9	10	○	☆ make offerings to gods; housecleaning *3rd Dog Days period* ✘ marriage; end mourning; launch business
Th	10	11	○	☆ study; visit; house building; make offerings ✘ visit fortune teller; mourning; repair fishing nets
Fr	11	12	○	☆ sea cruise; hunt; fish; amusements; adopt pets ✘ make wine; make preserves; christen boat
Sa	12	13	●	☆ unlucky day: no activities ✘ dig canals; make offerings to ancestors; pray for fertility
Su	13	14	○	☆ make offerings; visit; marriage; give dowries; hairstyling ✘ legal trial; dig wells; lay foundations
Mo	14	15	●	☆ make offerings; study; dinner party; sign contracts ✘ deliver goods; funerals
Tu	15	16	○	☆ visit; marriage; prepare for marriage; adoption ✘ sow crops; travel; end mourning
We	16	17	●	☆ study; travel; marriage; give dowries ✘ kitchen work; paint walls
Th	17	18	○	☆ engagements; house building; paint walls ✘ hairstyling; swim; acupuncture; move house
Fr	18	19	○	☆ travel; visiting; marriage; housecleaning; medical check ✘ prepare wedding bed; buy property
Sa	19	20	○	☆ hairstyling; house building; mourning; funerals ✘ sow crops; irrigation; prendre le bateau
Su	20	21	●	☆ unlucky day: no activities ✘ repair fishing nets; mourning
Mo	21	22	○	☆ repair paths; make offerings, swim; paint walls ✘ marriage; make wine; funerals
Tu	22	23	○	☆ make offerings; visit friends; marriage; house building ✘ irrigation; drain water; funerals
We	23	24	○	☆ travel; engagements; building work ❑ Limit of Heat ✘ legal trial; move house
Th	24	25	●	☆ unlucky day: no activities ✘ make offerings; deliver goods; move house
Fr	25	26	○	☆ marriage; hairstyling; prepare for marriage; funerals ✘ sow crops; dig wells; install faucets
Sa	26	27	●	☆ study; new clothes; engagements; house raising ✘ kitchen work; install furnaces
Su	27	28	○	☆ visit; marriage; give dowries; open shop ✘ house building; hairstyling; travel; dig wells
Mo	28	29	●	☆ study; visit; travel; house building ✘ bathroom work; buy property or land
Tu	29	VIII	○	☆ engagements; lay foundations; paint walls ✘ kitchen work; install furnaces; pray for fertility
We	30	2	○	☆ travel; new clothes; housecleaning; adopt pets ✘ prepare wedding bed; building foundations
Th	31	3	○	☆ make offerings; hairstyling; house building; funerals ✘ make wine; make preserves; hunt

● lucky day   ○ neutral day   ● unlucky day   ❑ 24 solar terms
☆ auspicious activity   ✘ inauspicious activity

154

SEPTEMBER 2000 / 8th month of the Dragon year

Fr	1	4	●	☆ unlucky day: no activities ✖ funerals; end mourning; hunt; fish; make offerings
Sa	2	5	○	☆ paint walls; swim; paint walls; make offerings ✖ legal trial; marriage; pray for fertility; marriage
Su	3	6	●	☆ make offerings; visit; marriage; new clothes; house building ✖ mourning; deliver goods; sow crops
Mo	4	7	○	☆ visit friends; adopt pets; travel; hunt ✖ sow crops; sign contracts; move house
Tu	5	8	●	☆ unlucky day: no activities ✖ kitchen work; make offerings; pray for fertility
We	6	9	○	☆ travel; marriage; give dowries; house raising; funerals ✖ hairstyling; dig wells; install faucets
Th	7	10	●	☆ engagements; funerals; study ❑ White Dew ✖ legal trial; buy property or land; irrigation
Fr	8	11	○	☆ study; marriage; give dowries; medical check ✖ travel; christen boat; funerals
Sa	9	12	○	☆ make offerings; acupuncture; travel; hunt; fish ✖ bathroom work; repair fishing nets
Su	10	13	●	☆ travel; study; marriage; house raising ✖ make wine; make preserves; house building
Mo	11	14	○	☆ hairstyling; housecleaning; repair granary; funerals ✖ prepare wedding bed; building waterworks
Tu	12	15	○	☆ make offerings; funerals *Mid-Autumn Festival* ✖ legal trial; house building; cut trees; funerals
We	13	16	●	☆ unlucky day: no activities ✖ funerals; deliver goods; visit friends
Th	14	17	○	☆ study; visit friends; house building ✖ marriage; end mourning; hunt; fish
Fr	15	18	○	☆ build footpaths; swim; make offerings ✖ kitchen work; install furnaces; hunt
Sa	16	19	●	☆ study; travel; marriage; funerals ✖ hairstyling; new clothes; buy houses
Su	17	20	○	☆ visit; house building; kitchen work; funerals ✖ make offerings; buy property; funerals
Mo	18	21	●	☆ unlucky day: no activities ✖ dig wells or ponds; install faucets
Tu	19	22	○	☆ visit; marriage; give dowries; funerals ✖ deliver goods; repair fishing nets
We	20	23	○	☆ make offerings; marriage; new clothes; immigration ✖ make wine; christen boat; travel
Th	21	24	○	☆ hairstyling; hunt; amusements; do not visit the sick ✖ irrigation work; christen boat
Fr	22	25	●	☆ unlucky day: no activities ✖ legal trial; house building; sign contracts
Sa	23	26	○	☆ travel; funerals; swim ❑ Autumn Equinox ✖ acupuncture; prepare wedding bed
Su	24	27	○	☆ swim; housecleaning; buy houses or property ✖ sow crops; house building; lay foundations
Mo	25	28	●	☆ unlucky day: no activities ✖ kitchen work; funerals; make wine
Tu	26	29	○	☆ visit; travel; immigration; paint walls ✖ hairstyling; marriage; end mourning; sea travel; funerals
We	27	30	○	☆ build footpath; irrigation work ✖ buy land or property; pray for happiness
Th	28	IX	○	☆ make offerings; marriage; give dowries; house building ✖ sow crops; end mourning
Fr	29	2	○	☆ study; travel; engagements; house building ✖ make offerings to ancestors; repair fishing nets
Sa	30	3	●	☆ unlucky day: no activities ✖ dig wells; make wine; make preserves

● lucky day   ○ neutral day   ● unlucky day   ❑ 24 solar terms
☆ auspicious activity   ✖ inauspicious activity

155

OCTOBER 2000 / *9th month of the Dragon year*

Day				Activities
Su	1	4	○	☆ immigration; marriage; hairstyling; house building ✘ repair granary; build dikes; irrigation
Mo	2	5	●	☆ make offerings; study; marriage; medical check ✘ travel; mourning; funerals; lay foundations
Tu	3	6	○	☆ marriage; hairstyling; travel; hunt; fish ✘ bathroom work; deliver goods
We	4	7	○	☆ study; marriage; give dowries; new clothes ✘ sow crops; end mourning; house building; dig wells
Th	5	8	○	☆ travel; housecleaning; hairstyling; adopt pets ✘ prepare wedding bed; kitchen work
Fr	6	9	○	☆ make offerings; swim; housecleaning *Double 9 Festival* ✘ hairstyling; lay foundations; new clothes; engagements
Sa	7	10	●	☆ unlucky day: no activities ✘ buy property; funerals; acupuncture
Su	8	11	○	☆ hairstyling; housecleaning ❑ Cold Dew ✘ marriage; lay foundations; move house
Mo	9	12	○	☆ make offerings; study; hunt; acupuncture ✘ repair fishing nets; christen boat
Tu	10	13	○	☆ make offerings; repair fishing nets; paint walls ✘ make wine; house building; receive payment
We	11	14	●	☆ building foundations; mourning; funerals ✘ make offerings; build waterworks; medical check
Th	12	15	●	☆ make offerings; visit friends; marriage; give dowries; funerals ✘ deliver goods; dig wells; receive payment
Fr	13	16	●	☆ unlucky day: no activities ✘ receive payment; deliver goods; funerals
Sa	14	17	○	☆ marriage; give dowry; prepare for marriage; hunt ✘ travel; sow crops; pray for happiness
Su	15	18	●	☆ study; marriage; medical check; funerals ✘ kitchen work; install furnaces; bathroom work
Mo	16	19	○	☆ travel; hunt; fish ✘ hairstyling; irrigation work; sea travel
Tu	17	20	●	☆ study; visit; travel; marriage ✘ buy property; mourning; prepare for marriage
We	18	21	○	☆ hairstyling; building in kitchen; funerals ✘ acupuncture; end mourning; install home appliances
Th	19	22	●	☆ unlucky day: no activities ✘ funerals; lay foundations; cut trees
Fr	20	23	○	☆ make offerings; study; travel; hairstyling; house raising ✘ make wine; marriage; house building
Sa	21	24	○	☆ travel; visit; hairstyling; new clothes; funerals ✘ dig canals; drain water; visit friends
Su	22	25	●	☆ unlucky day: no activities ✘ legal trial; fish; marriage; move house
Mo	23	26	●	☆ visit; funerals ❑ First Frost ✘ make offerings; travel; pray for fertility
Tu	24	27	○	☆ travel; hunt; prepare wedding bed ✘ sow crops; dig wells; move house
We	25	28	●	☆ unlucky day: no activities ✘ kitchen work; install furnaces; hairstyling
Th	26	29	○	☆ make offerings; engagements; prepare wedding bed ✘ hairstyling; travel; pray for happiness; house building
Fr	27	X	●	☆ study; marriage; give dowries; house raising ✘ buy land; end mourning; funerals
Sa	28	2	○	☆ travel; hunt; fish ✘ end mourning; marriage; engagements; receive payment
Su	29	3	○	☆ travel; hairstyling; house building; immigration ✘ prepare wedding bed; repair fishing nets
Mo	30	4	○	☆ hairstyling; housecleaning; kitchen work; funerals ✘ make wine; acupuncture; hunt; fish
Tu	31	5	●	☆ make offerings; housecleaning; visit friends; adoption ✘ irrigation work; house building

● lucky day   ○ neutral day   ● unlucky day   ❑ 24 solar terms
☆ auspicious activity   ✘ inauspicious activity

NOVEMBER 2000 / *10th month of the Dragon year*

We	1	6	○	☆ hairstyling; housecleaning; medical check; house raising ✘ marriage; lay foundations; funerals
Th	2	7	○	☆ make offerings; study; visit friends; travel ✘ visit fortune teller; deliver goods; hairstyling
Fr	3	8	○	☆ kitchen work; install furnaces; paint walls ✘ sow crops; deliver goods
Sa	4	9	●	☆ end mourning; visit friends; funerals ✘ make offerings to ancestors; kitchen work; funerals
Su	5	10	●	☆ make offerings; visit friends; travel; marriage; adoption ✘ hairstyling; dig wells; sign contracts
Mo	6	11	○	☆ unlucky day: no activities ✘ buy houses or land; pray for fertility
Tu	7	12	●	☆ unlucky day: no activities ❏ Beginning of Winter ✘ end mourning; travel; visit friends; give dowries
We	8	13	○	☆ marriage; give dowries; house building; funerals ✘ bathroom work; repair fishing nets
Th	9	14	○	☆ study; marriage; adoption; funerals ✘ make wine; make preserves; adopt a child
Fr	10	15	○	☆ make offerings; housecleaning; travel; hunt; fish ✘ irrigation work; prepare wedding bed
Sa	11	16	○	☆ hairstyling; house building; kitchen work ✘ cut trees; legal trial; make wine
Su	12	17	●	☆ unlucky day: no activities ✘ receive payment; deliver goods; acupuncture
Mo	13	18	○	☆ make offerings; sortie; hairstyling; house building ✘ marriage; sow crops; buy houses; acupuncture
Tu	14	19	○	☆ engagements; new clothes; house raising; funerals ✘ visit fortune teller; install furnaces; fish
We	15	20	○	☆ make offerings; visit friends; paint walls ✘ hairstyling; funerals
Th	16	21	○	☆ marriage; give dowries; immigration; funerals ✘ make offerings; lay foundations; pray for happiness
Fr	17	22	●	☆ make offerings; study; travel; marriage ✘ dig wells or ponds; do not visit the sick
Sa	18	23	○	☆ visit friends; marriage; new clothes; funerals ✘ repair fishing nets; lay foundations
Su	19	24	●	☆ unlucky day: no activities ✘ make wine; travel; marriage; engagements;
Mo	20	25	○	☆ engagements; hairstyling; lay foundations; kitchen work ✘ bathroom work; irrigation; sign contracts
Tu	21	26	○	☆ make offerings; study; engagements; funerals ✘ legal trial; install furnaces; kitchen work
We	22	27	○	☆ marriage; hairstyling; immigration ❏ Slight Snow ✘ receive payment; prepare wedding bed
Th	23	28	●	☆ marriage; study; house building; immigration ✘ sow crops; visit friends; cut trees; hunt
Fr	24	29	●	☆ unlucky day: no activities ✘ kitchen work; install furnaces
Sa	25	30	○	☆ make offerings to ancestors; swim ✘ marriage; lay foundations; house building
Su	26	XI	●	☆ swim; housecleaning; travel; new clothes; house building ✘ buy houses or land; pray for fertility; give dowries
Mo	27	2	○	☆ paint walls; install furnaces; open stores ✘ end mourning; funerals; cut trees; sow crops
Tu	28	3	○	☆ travel; marriage; give dowries; hairstyling; funerals ✘ make offerings; pray for happiness; repair fishing nets
We	29	4	○	☆ study; marriage; immigration; funerals ✘ make wine; dig wells or ponds; building work
Th	30	5	○	☆ study; hairstyling; marriage; new clothes ✘ dig canals; lay foundations; do business

● lucky day   ○ neutral day   ● unlucky day   ❏ 24 solar terms
☆ auspicious activity   ✘ inauspicious activity

157

DECEMBER 2000 / *11th month of the Dragon year*

Fr	1	6	●	☆ unlucky day: no activities ✖ legal trial; travel; visit friends; funerals
Sa	2	7	●	☆ make offerings; marriage; give dowries; immigrate; lay foundations ✖ christen boat; deliver goods
Su	3	8	●	☆ make offerings; study; engagements; funerals ✖ sow crops; hunt; fish; travel
Mo	4	9	○	☆ swim; housecleaning; travel; hunt; take care with knives ✖ kitchen work; prepare wedding bed
Tu	5	10	○	☆ make offerings; study; travel; lay foundations ✖ hairstyling; new clothes; make wine
We	6	11	●	☆ unlucky day: no activities ✖ buy houses or land; travel; engagements
Th	7	12	○	☆ paint walls; interior decoration ☐ Great Snow ✖ marriage; end mourning; funerals; lay foundations
Fr	8	13	○	☆ paint walls; move house; manicure babies ✖ lay foundations; repair fishing nets
Sa	9	14	●	☆ make offerings; travel; marriage; housecleaning; funerals ✖ end mourning; make wine
Su	10	15	○	☆ study; travel; marriage; kitchen work ✖ irrigation; drain water; make offerings
Mo	11	16	○	☆ make offerings; hunt; fish; receive payment ✖ legal trial; dig wells; prepare for marriage
Tu	12	17	●	☆ visit friends; travel; marriage; open stores ✖ deliver goods; christen boat
We	13	18	○	☆ immigration; buy houses; house building ✖ sow crops; end mourning; travel; engagements
Th	14	19	●	☆ unlucky day: no activities ✖ kitchen work; install furnaces; pray for fertility
Fr	15	20	○	☆ make offerings; cut trees ✖ hairstyling; new clothes; marriage; engagements;
Sa	16	21	●	☆ study; marriage; medical check; funerals ✖ buy houses; lay foundations; sow crops
Su	17	22	○	☆ hairstyling; manicure babies; travel; hunt; fish ✖ kitchen work; install furnaces
Mo	18	23	●	☆ unlucky day: no activities ✖ christen boat; install home appliances
Tu	19	24	○	☆ prepare wedding bed; kitchen work ✖ make wine; marriage; acupuncture
We	20	25	●	☆ unlucky day: no activities ✖ irrigation work; lay foundations; move house
Th	21	26	○	☆ make offerings; engagements; hairstyling ☐ Winter Solstice ✖ legal trial; end mourning
Fr	22	27	○	☆ study; visit; new clothes; funerals ✖ make offerings; deliver goods; medical check
Sa	23	28	○	☆ make offerings; hunt; fish; do not visit the sick ✖ sow crops; dig wells; visit; adopt a child
Su	24	29	●	☆ make offerings; visit; marriage; new clothes ✖ kitchen work; sow crops
Mo	25	30	○	☆ buy houses; interior decoration *Christmas* ✖ hairstyling; travel; marriage; funerals
Tu	26	XII	●	☆ unlucky day: no activities ✖ buy houses or land; travel; move house
We	27	1	●	☆ hairstyling; prepare wedding bed; irrigation ✖ sea travel; fish; make wine
Th	28	2	○	☆ pray for happiness; visit friends; new clothes ✖ prepare wedding bed; christen boat
Fr	29	3	○	☆ hairstyling; new clothes; housecleaning; hunt ✖ make wine; lay foundations
Sa	30	4	●	☆ unlucky day: no activities ✖ irrigation; drain water; adopt a child
Su	31	5	○	☆ house building; kitchen work; swim; manicure babies ✖ marriage; acupuncture; funerals

● lucky day ○ neutral day ● unlucky day ☐ 24 solar terms
☆ auspicious activity ✖ inauspicious activity

158

Day				Activities
Mo	1	7	●	☆ make offerings to ancestors; swim; sign contracts ✖ pray for happiness; marriage; lay foundations
Tu	2	8	○	☆ make offerings; visit friends; travel; marriage; new clothes ✖ sow crops; mourning
We	3	9	○	☆ install home appliances; sow crops; sign contracts ✖ make offerings; engagements; move house; kitchen work
Th	4	10	●	☆ make offerings; garden work; repair paths ✖ hairstyling; dig wells; prepare wedding bed
Fr	5	11	○	☆ swim; manicure babies; housecleaning ❒ Slight Cold ✖ travel; prepare wedding bed; buy land
Sa	6	12	○	☆ visit friends; marriage; house raising; adopt pets ✖ travel; sow crops; paint walls
Su	7	13	○	☆ make offerings; marriage; move house; funerals ✖ install home appliances; hunt; fish
Mo	8	14	●	☆ unlucky day: no activities ✖ lay foundations; funerals; make wine
Tu	9	15	○	☆ make offerings; open stores; adopt pets ✖ visit friends; prepare wedding bed
We	10	16	●	☆ lunar eclipse; unlucky day: no activities ✖ legal trial; demolition; lay foundations
Th	11	17	○	☆ make offerings to gods and ancestors; housecleaning ✖ hairstyling; new clothes; move house; receive payment
Fr	12	18	●	☆ study; pray for fertility; house raising ✖ travel; engagements; give dowries; cut trees
Sa	13	19	○	☆ make offerings; new clothes; adopt pets ✖ open stores; adopt a child; do business
Su	14	20	○	☆ make offerings; sign contracts; do business ✖ pray for fertility; funerals; receive payment
Mo	15	21	●	☆ study; engagements; kitchen work ✖ make offerings; travel; lay foundations; funerals
Tu	16	22	○	☆ make offerings; receive payment; engagements; study ✖ dig wells; visit friends; marriage; give dowries
We	17	23	○	☆ marriage; make offerings; build footpaths ✖ move house; prepare wedding bed
Th	18	24	●	☆ make offerings; visit friends; engagements; adopt pets ✖ make wine; sow crops; travel; funerals
Fr	19	25	○	☆ travel; swim; hairstyling; hunt; funerals ✖ house raising; install home appliances; open stores
Sa	20	26	●	☆ unlucky day: no activities ❒ Great Cold ✖ engagements; marriage; sign contracts; legal trial
Su	21	27	○	☆ make offerings; travel; new clothes; hairstyling; house raising ✖ engagements; prepare wedding bed
Mo	22	28	○	☆ study; marriage; repair granary ✖ hunt; fish; sow crops; plantation
Tu	23	29	●	☆ unlucky day: no activities ✖ kitchen work; hairstyling; deliver goods
We	24	1	●	☆ make offerings; swim; study Year of the Snake begins ✖ open stores; sign contracts
Th	25	2	●	☆ make offerings; swim; move house; sign contracts ✖ travel; acupuncture; do business
Fr	26	3	○	☆ new clothes; set up altar ✖ marriage; hunt; fish; funerals
Sa	27	4	○	☆ visit friends; engagements; house raising; funerals ✖ make offerings; deliver goods
Su	28	5	○	☆ make offerings; adopt a child; install home appliances ✖ new clothes; lay foundations; house raising
Mo	29	6	○	☆ interior decoration; build footpaths ✖ make offerings to ancestors; lay foundations; building work
Tu	30	7	○	☆ engagements; new clothes; make wine ✖ travel; end mourning; funerals
We	31	8	●	☆ make offerings; swim; new clothes; hunt; cut trees ✖ move house; install home appliances; make wine

● lucky day   ○ neutral day   ● unlucky day   ❒ 24 solar terms
☆ auspicious activity   ✖ inauspicious activity

Books
from
Asia 2000

Non-fiction

Behind the Brushstrokes – Appreciating Chinese Calligraphy	Khoo & Penrose
Cantonese Culture	Shirley Ingram & Rebecca Ng
Concise World Atlas	Maps International
Egg Woman's Daughter	Mary Chan
Farewell, My Colony	Todd Crowell
Getting Along With the Chinese	Fred Schneiter
The Great Red Hope	Jonathan Eley
Hong Kong, Macau and the Muddy Pearl	Annabel Jackson
Hong Kong Pathfinder	Martin Williams
Hyundai	Donald Kirk
Macau's Gardens and Landscape Art	Cabral, Jackson & Leung
Quaille's Practical Chinese-English Dictionary	
Red Chips and the Globalisation of China's Enterprises	Charles de Trenck
The Rise & Decline of the Asian Century	Christopher Lingle
Tokyo: City on the Edge Todd Crowell & Stephanie Forman Morimura	
Walking to the Mountain	Wendy Teasdill

Fiction

Cheung Chau Dog Fanciers' Society	Alan B Pierce
Chinese Opera	Alex Kuo
Chinese Walls	Xu Xi
Daughters of Hui	Xu Xi
Getting to Lamma	Jan Alexander
The Ghost Locust	Heather Stroud
Hong Kong Rose	Xu Xi
Last Seen in Shanghai	Howard Turk
Riding a Tiger	Robert Abel
Shanghai	Christopher New
Temutma	Rebecca Bradley & Stewart Sloan

Poetry

An Amorphous Melody	Kavita
The Last Beach	Mani Rao
New Ends, Old Beginnings	Louise Ho
Round – Poems and Photographs of Asia	Slavick & Baker
Woman to Woman and other poems	Agnes Lam

Order from Asia 2000 Ltd
302 Seabird House, 22–28 Wyndham St, Central, Hong Kong
tel (852) 2530-1409; fax (852) 2526-1107
email sales@asia2000.com.hk; http://www.asia2000.com.hk/